PASTRY TEMPLE

PASTRY

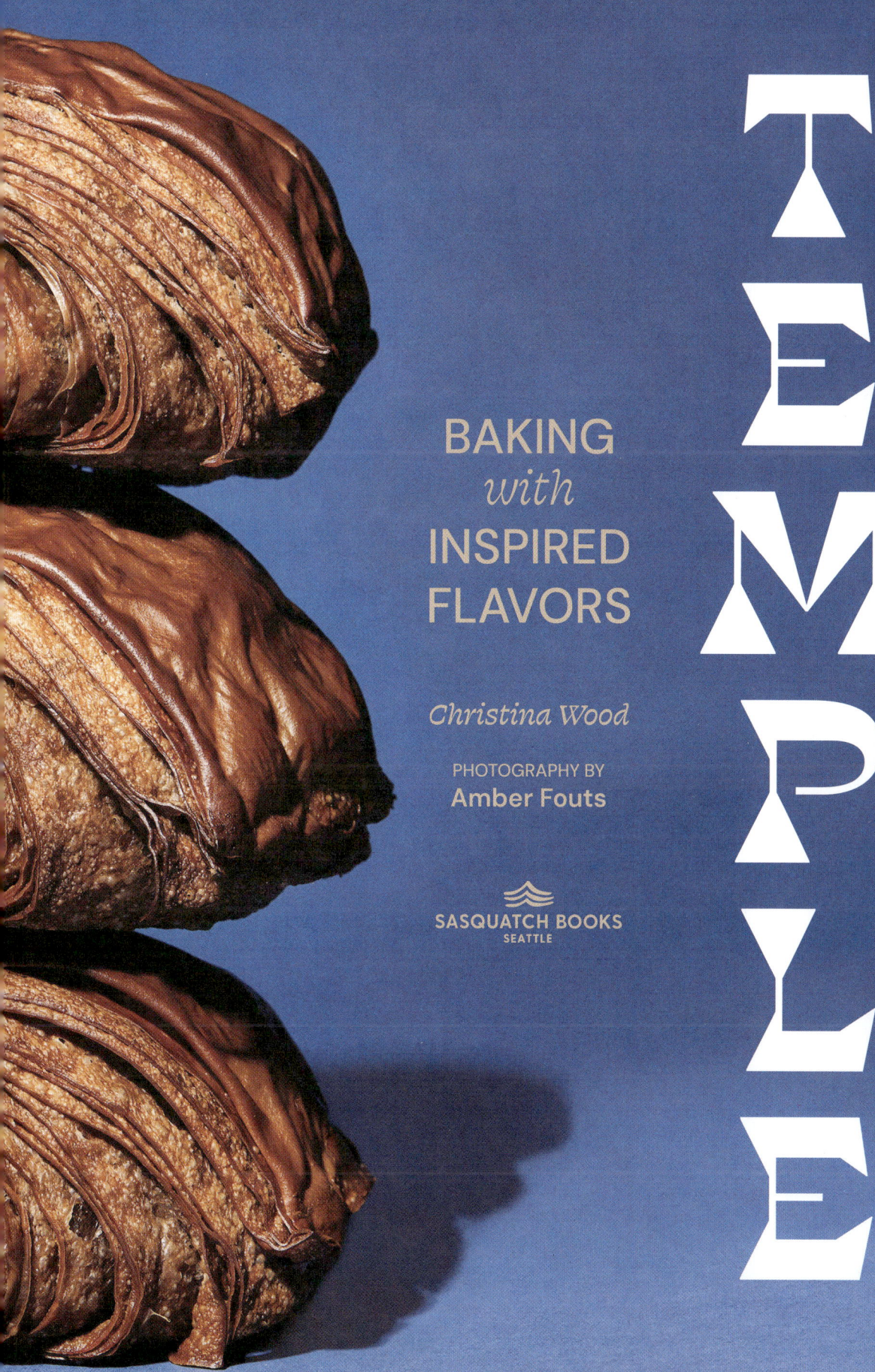

BAKING
with
INSPIRED
FLAVORS

Christina Wood

PHOTOGRAPHY BY
Amber Fouts

SASQUATCH BOOKS
SEATTLE

TEMPLE

The Three Pillars

BRIOCHE

Building an Altar to Pastry

When you enter my bakery, Temple Pastries, you immediately know you're in a pious place. It has soaring ceilings, a soft echo off the concrete floors, and giant windows flooding the white walls and cascading plants with light, even on the darkest of Seattle winter days. This interior reflects my dedication to and reverence for pastry. A perfectly executed croissant, an unbelievably light morsel of brioche—these are my reasons for being, my calling. But I don't come from a long line of pastry chefs or gourmands, so how did I get here?

I must first tell you about the tulips. I spent my childhood on a rural Midwestern stretch of land surrounded by woods and bordered by a wide, slow-moving river. I spent as much time as I possibly could outside, roaming the forest, getting to know the habits of the little snakes and bunnies and birds that lived there, committing to memory every tree, every glen, every ring of mushrooms that sprang up. There was a giant maple tree that stood alone in the middle of a field that I had a certain affection for. Half of it had been incinerated in a bonfire that got out of control, but the other half was just as alive as ever. At the base of this tree, a handful of tulips popped up every spring. There were no other flowers on the property apart from the usual dandelions and lawn daisies, and this little outcropping of maybe eight individual tulips appearing each year seemed to me like magic. Each spring I anticipated seeing them, and when they finally arrived, it felt special, like nature had built an altar to honor this beautiful place I loved.

While I may have been a free-spirited romantic on my own time, my home life was quite the opposite. I grew up in an extremely Protestant home. My life was structured around church and hard work. It was expected of me to show my dedication to God by keeping on the straight and narrow path, getting straight A's in school, participating in sports, and attending Sunday school and all manner of extracurricular church activities. Self-discipline, structure, and piety were the cornerstones of my upbringing. Earthly pleasures were seen as frivolous, since our true reward of heaven was waiting for us in the afterlife. As a child, I honestly didn't hate this, but I lived in constant fear of disappointing God and my parents. My love affair with the tulips was a strictly private matter, one I buried within myself.

It wasn't until my early twenties that I started to break free from this fundamental upbringing. I was living in Gainesville, Florida, under the pretense of getting an accounting degree, but really I was doing all the things I wasn't allowed to do growing up. As I met more people outside the church community, I realized there was a whole world of experiences and ideas I had never encountered. I was enthralled! I came out as queer. I started reading feminist literature. My friends were artists and musicians and punks and anarchists. The structure and self-discipline I had learned and lived up to that point seemed to serve no purpose, and I threw them away with abandon to pursue a creative life. Those tulips were calling to me, a promise of deeper meaning and connection that I had been missing, and now I could live it out in the open.

It was during this phase of my life that I discovered baking. I had never had an interest in food before (see above re: earthly pleasures), but my best friend had started getting me into cooking, and from there, I ventured to the sweet side of the kitchen and fell in love. It had never occurred to me that I could choose a career path that wasn't traditional, practical, and guaranteed to make me a comfortable suburban living. Dry, rule-based accounting wasn't really doing it for me. But baking? Now *that* sounded like the perfect career choice. I began dreaming up cakes and pies and cookies in my head, letting my imagination run wild. But because I was so focused on the creative aspects and had no foundation in the rules of baking, I had many, many failed concepts. One that stands out in my memory is a brownie recipe I tried to make vegan, and I ended up with an inedible brick of baked cocoa-avocado paste! I began to realize that pure creativity without a solid base of skill would only lead to continued failure. So I hunted down anything and everything I could find about the rules and science of baking and practiced at home as often as I could. This was the beginning of something, I could tell, a path to the future I wanted for myself. I supposed the next step was to get a job at a bakery, so I dropped off a paltry résumé and a loaf of home-baked challah at a place in town. That was enough to get me the job.

1

2

3

4

I threw myself into that work. I was granted a lot of creative control and made an ever-changing menu of weekly cake and pastry specials alongside the hand-mixed sourdough breads we made there. I picked up swing shifts just to learn new things and asked a million questions to find out *why* instead of just *how,* and I soon realized my thirst for knowledge would not be quenched in a college-town bakery. It was time to take the next, most terrifying step: move to a real city. I thought Seattle sounded nice. One of my friends was planning a move to Portland, so I sold all my stuff and jumped in his car with a suitcase, a very small nest egg, and a dream. I didn't know anyone in Seattle, had never stepped foot in it or even looked at it on a map, but all signs pointed to this being the right move.

As luck (or fate) would have it, I landed a job at a well-known bakery run by an award-winning chef, and all sorts of gaps in my knowledge were filled in. It was apparent my skill level was behind most people who worked there; I didn't go to culinary school or have years of experience. The pressure was on; this was my sink or swim moment. I pushed myself so hard I would come home and cry at the end of the day just to let it all out. It was in this environment that I came back to what was instilled in me as a kid: self-discipline, structure, and piety—but this time for pastry.

These qualities that I abandoned to do some necessary self-discovery and healing were exactly what I needed to revisit, not because I was afraid of the consequences of not living that way, but because I was excited about what I could accomplish and create using those tools. I worked with intention every day. I treated my jobs like school. I still read everything I could find regarding pastry and bread. And while I studied, I didn't try to bury my creative pursuits but instead treasured them, so when I branched out on my own, there was a deep well of inspiration to dip into, along with the skill level to pull it off. The art of pastry is what brought me fully into myself. I have reemerged, a blooming tulip, building an altar to the place I love: my very own pastry temple.

How to Use This Book

This book is meant to be the exact book I was searching for when I was learning how to make pastry on my own. It's not difficult to find inspirational and creative baking books, but what I really wanted to know was the theory and technical skill behind the creativity. There are three basic pastry doughs covered in this book, what I refer to as the Three Pillars of Pastry: brioche, puff pastry, and croissant. With these doughs, you can make so many different pastries, and when mastered, they create a very solid foundation to build on. Each section will begin with a pillar recipe. This will include theory and technical know-how for executing that dough. I highly recommend you practice the pillar recipes before moving on to the more embellished recipes that follow. Following the pillar recipes, you'll find savory and sweet applications for each dough and inspirational and creative ways to use them. You can follow these exactly or use them as a jumping-off point for your own creative pursuits!

Each recipe has not only ingredients and methods listed but also a timeline. Baking requires a lot of planning ahead, and all of these recipes span at least two days, some of them more. But don't worry, it's not all active time! Most of it is waiting for fermentation or resting the dough. Make sure you pay attention to the timeline before beginning so you don't get jammed up.

Most importantly, do not stress over things being perfect! Working in a home environment is going to result in pastries with personality, so embrace each bake's certain *je ne sais quoi*. That's part of the fun of it: picking up on all the nuances of your ingredients, your technique, and your environment. If something happens to go undeniably wrong, there is a section at the end for troubleshooting.

Before You Begin

If you've ever opened a cookbook, you know the first thing any of them talk about is how important it is to choose the right ingredients. I remember back in my rule-bucking days, I would *roll my damn eyes* every time I read that section. Now that I am older and wiser and love following rules, let me plead with you to take this section to heart.

Ingredients

I do not know any other application in which the ingredients play a more crucial role than in baking. Flours, butters, yeasts, and chocolates vary widely in quality and performance, and with so few ingredients going into a dough, the ingredients *actually matter a lot*. Here, you will find my *highly* recommended brands to use.

BUTTER Always use unsalted butter—for these recipes and in life. All recipes in this book require a European-style butter with at least 82 percent butterfat. My preferred brand is Plugrà, but you can also use Kerrygold or any other higher-end butter. Do not cheap out on this ingredient! The reason it is so important to use this type of butter is because if there is more water content in the butter, it will break and become brittle instead of flexible, and you need flexible butter when you're laminating. Also more fat = more flavor!

CHOCOLATE Any high-quality, 100 percent real chocolate will work for these recipes. I typically go for a slightly dark but not too acidic or bitter chocolate, somewhere in the range of 55 to 65 percent cocoa. Some preferred brands include Valrhona, Cacao Barry, Guittard, and Callebaut. For cocoa powder, I use brute cocoa, also known as Dutch processed, which means it is alkalized, is not natural, and is less bitter than non-Dutched cocoa.

FLOUR Flour may be the most crucial ingredient in these recipes, so it is important to choose the right one. For brioche and croissant recipes, I use King Arthur Bread Flour. This is widely available in most supermarkets. Bread flour is required to create the necessary gluten structure needed to support all the fats and sugars in the doughs, whereas all-purpose or cake flour lacks the protein content to create those structures. For puff pastry, I use King Arthur All-Purpose Flour because it makes a slightly softer and more tender dough.

GELATIN Some dessert elements in this book require gelatin. You must get silver-strength sheet gelatin, not the powdered kind. They do not have the same strength, and they work differently. You can find sheet gelatin at specialty baking stores and online. To bloom sheet gelatin, place the sheets in ice water until they are soft (takes 3 to 5 minutes), then squeeze excess water out of them. They are then ready to use and will melt easily in hot liquid.

MILK All recipes require full-fat whole milk, preferably organic or grass fed for the best flavor. Look at your local farmers' market or natural food stores for high-quality dairy products.

SALT I use fine sea salt in all recipes. Since the volume of salt varies widely between textures and brands, be sure to weigh your salt.

SUGAR Unless otherwise specified, use white granulated sugar. For some recipes I will call for demerara sugar, which I like for its darker taste and coarse texture. For the Tropézienne recipe (page 71), I call for white pearl sugar, which is a specialty sugar that does not melt in the oven and can be found in specialty baking stores or online.

VANILLA EXTRACT Always use real vanilla extract, not imitation. I prefer Nielsen-Massey for its robust flavor.

YEAST Use any brand labeled dry active yeast (not instant or fresh).

Equipment

A small collection of inexpensive tools will make all the difference in your kitchen. Here is some necessary equipment to have on hand for most recipes. Many recipes require special equipment, and that will be listed above the ingredients of each recipe.

- Baking sheets (a.k.a. half-sheet pans)
- Instant-read thermometer
- Kitchen scale that can measure grams
- Metal bench scraper
- Oven thermometer
- Parchment paper
- Pastry brush
- Plastic wrap
- Proofing box (see page 26 for work-arounds if you don't have one)
- Rolling pin
- Stand mixer with hook, whisk, and paddle attachments
- Yardstick ruler or tape measure

NOTE Plastic wrap from the grocery store can be a huge pain to work with, getting stuck on itself, becoming near impossible to tear from the roll, ending in frustration. I know it's not just me! I recommend buying a roll from a restaurant supply store. Many of them are open to the public, and they sell 12-inch rolls. It will last forever, is not much more expensive than the small rolls at the grocery store, and will be so much easier to use!

The following section will go over in detail how to perform some basic processes that are used over and over again in this book. Please reference them whenever needed.

Making a Butter Block

For puff pastry and croissant doughs, you'll need to laminate them with a butter block. Make the butter block the day before. Cut 500 grams of room-temperature butter into roughly 1-inch cubes and lightly dust with flour (photo 1).

Place them close together on a piece of parchment paper and cover with a piece of plastic wrap. Use your hands and then a rolling pin to smash the butter cubes together; let some aggression out here and really let 'er rip (photo 2)!

Now start rolling the butter out into a flat 8-by-8-inch square for puff or 10-by-7-inch rectangle for croissant (photo 3).

Use a metal bench scraper to make the corners squared off and pay special attention to making the entire thing very flat and of even thickness. You can lift the plastic wrap off and rearrange it as necessary to achieve this.

Keep it in the fridge and pull it out to come up to room temperature about 30 minutes to 1 hour before you need it, depending on the ambient temperature of your kitchen. When laminating with it, it should be cold but flexible (photo 4).

Locking in the Butter

With your butter block at room temperature now, you'll need to lock it in before laminating. You'll find a description and photos of the process on page 86 (for puff pastry) and on page 128 (for croissants).

Performing a Book Fold

The spine of the dough block should be to your left. Only roll toward you and away, not sideways or diagonally; you're just lengthening it, not widening it. Roll it to ⅓-inch thickness. If the short edges of your rectangle are not straight sides, use a paring knife to trim the edges so you end up with a rectangle shape. Do not trim the long sides of the rectangle.

- Rotate the dough so the long side is toward you and the spine is away from you (photo 1).
- Visually divide the dough into fourths, and fold both outer fourths to the middle, where they will meet (photo 2).
- Fold the right half over the left half (photo 3). The book fold is now completed (photo 4).

Performing a Letter Fold

With the spine in the dough on the left, start rolling the dough to lengthen it. You will only want to roll away from you and toward you, not sideways or diagonally; you're just lengthening it, not widening it. Roll it to ⅓-inch thickness. If the short edges of your rectangle are not straight sides, use a paring knife to trim the edges so you end up with a rectangle shape. Do not trim the long sides of the rectangle.

- Rotate the dough so the spine is away from you (photo 1).
- Visually divide the dough into thirds, and fold the left third over to cover the middle third (photo 2).
- Make sure the edges of the dough are lined up with each other. Then fold the right third over the middle third to finish your letter fold (photo 3).

BASIC PROCESSES

Egg Washing Pastries

Egg wash gives pastry its appealing shine. You'll want to apply it with a pastry brush and avoid pooling on the baking sheet. Your aim should be a thin layer evenly covering all exposed pastry. To make egg wash, mix 1 egg yolk and 2 tablespoons of heavy cream or milk together. Use immediately.

Scoring Pastries

Puff pastries are typically scored to allow for an even spring without tearing the dough apart. To properly score puff, you'll want to egg wash it first, and then use the tip of a sharp paring knife (or a razor blade) to cut partially through the dough in a decorative pattern. You want to avoid cutting all the way through the dough and also avoid not cutting deep enough. You're looking to go about halfway through it.

Filling Pastries

Several recipes here require you to fill a pastry with something. To do this, take a paring knife, poke the pastry where you want to fill it, and then twist it in a circular motion to bore a hole into the pastry. You can push the knife farther into a doughnut to create space for the filling, and for a croissant, you just need to bore through the bottom layer of pastry. To fill the pastry, insert the tip of your piping bag into the hole and give it a squeeze (see photo on opposite page). It can sometimes be deceiving when filling pastries. You'll think you're getting a ton of filling in there and then when you bite into it, nothing. To combat this, place the empty pastry on a scale and tare it out. Fill it, then put it back on the scale. You'll want 30 to 40 grams of filling.

Making a Scrap Dough Packet

When making puff pastry and croissants, you'll end up with a bit of trimmings and scraps. This dough should be kept! At the end of each of the pillar chapters, I've included a recipe to use with a scrap dough packet. To make one, collect your scraps and trimmings as you make them and keep them cold in the refrigerator, covered with plastic wrap so they don't dry out. When you have all you're going to make, take them to a very lightly floured surface and start pressing them together into a flat square or rectangular shape. Overlap them as needed to make sure there are no gaps. Once they're all laid out on each other, roll it very firmly with your rolling pin to secure all the pieces together. If it starts sticking to the counter, throw some flour down underneath it and try again. Give it a rest in the fridge for at least 30 minutes and up to 4 hours before rolling it out and making pastries with it. If your scrap packet isn't very big, you can wrap it in plastic and freeze it, then add to it the next time you make croissant or puff pastry dough again.

Wrapping and Storing Pastries

Pastries are best when eaten the same day, but if you have some left over that you want to save, wrap them tightly in plastic and keep them at room temperature. They can be refreshed in the oven before eating by putting them in at 350 degrees F for 5 minutes or until they're warmed through.

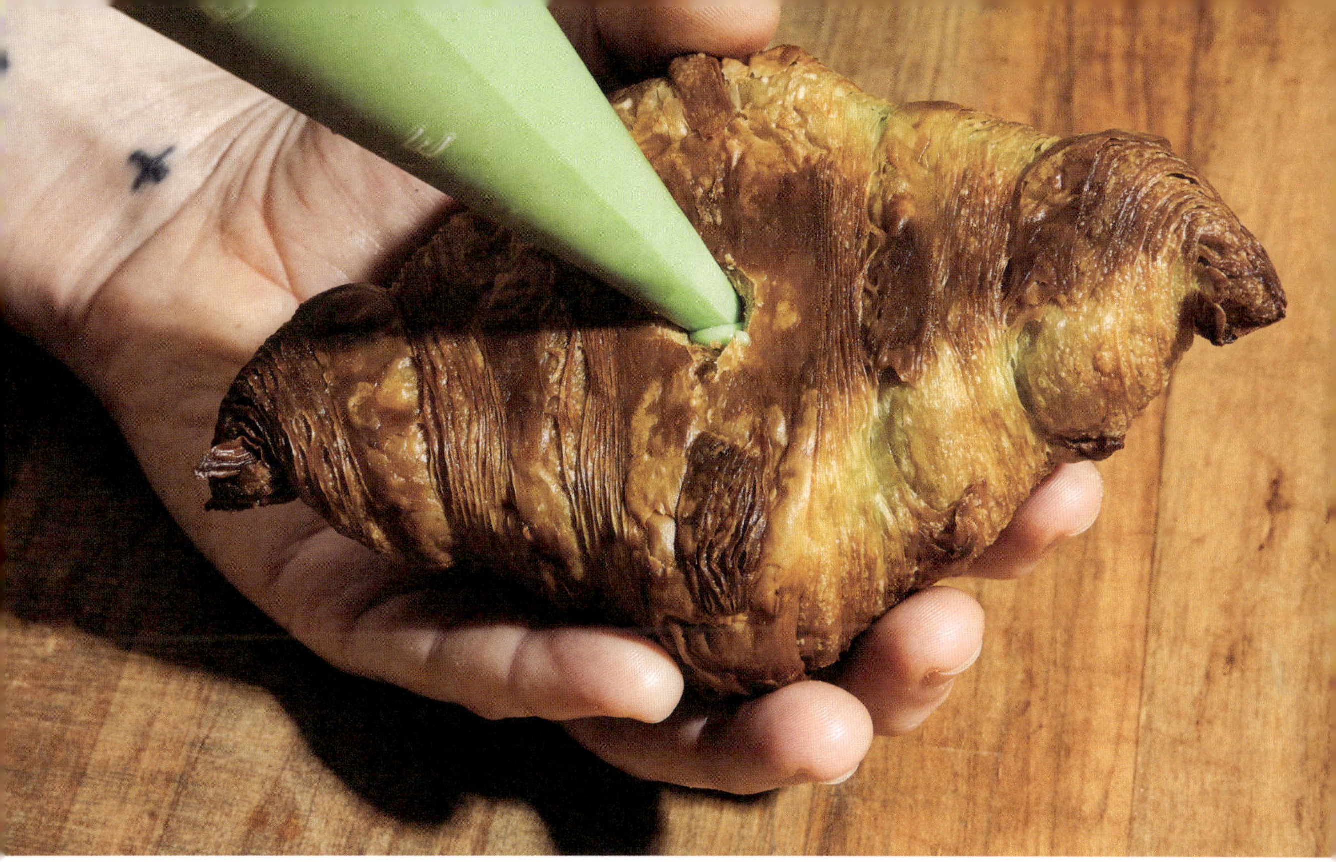

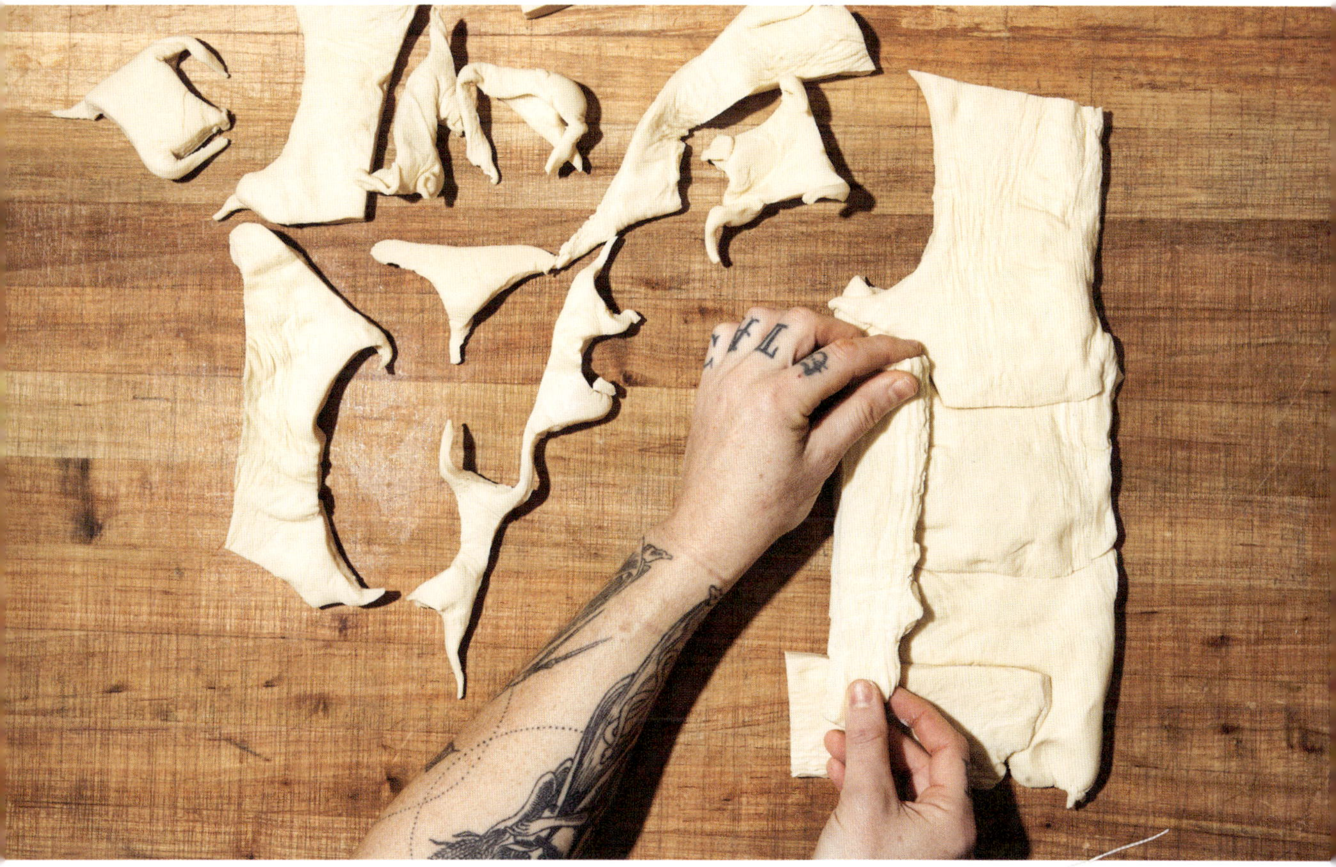

Proofing Pastries

Proper proofing of pastries is essential to success. Yeast is most active between 76 and 82 degrees F; this is quite a bit warmer than most home kitchens. If the temperature is too cold, proofing will take many hours, if it happens at all. If the temperature is too warm, butter will leak out of the dough before it is proofed, resulting in dry and greasy pastries. So how do you achieve this magical proofing environment? When I was recipe testing for my pop-ups, I bought a home proofing cabinet from Brød & Taylor that worked pretty well, and I'd recommend getting one if you plan to make lots of pastries at home.

If you don't want to invest in that, here's what I've found works best: Empty your dishwasher, and be prepared to leave it empty for at least two hours and up to four. Carefully place your tray of pastries in the top rack and put a baking sheet on the bottom rack. Place an empty bowl on the baking sheet. Bring a small pot of water (2 to 3 cups) to boil, then carefully pour it into the bowl and close the dishwasher door. Since your dishwasher is a completely closed environment, the steam from the water will keep the humidity up, and the warmth from it will help keep it warm but not too hot. If your kitchen is particularly cold, you may need to refresh the water once or twice, aiming to keep the internal temperature of the dishwasher in that golden range of 76 to 82 degrees F. You can also do this in the oven, but the water may need to be refreshed more often, as ovens are vented and won't trap the heat as well.

If you live in a hot environment or your kitchen is quite warm, you can proof pastries on the counter, lightly covered with plastic wrap. You may want to spritz the plastic wrap with cooking spray to make sure it doesn't stick to the pastries.

Knowing when pastries are proofed just the right amount is known as "calling proof," and it can be tricky. There are no hard and fast rules, and most professional bakers will tell you it's something you learn from experience. For brioche, I will gently poke the dough with my finger; it should feel aerated, like lots of tiny bubbles are in there, and slowly spring back; it will also be roughly doubled in size. If it springs back right away or feels dense, it's underproofed. If it doesn't spring back at all, it's overproofed.

My go-to for calling proof on croissants is to rapidly shake the baking sheet back and forth a small distance and watch how the pastries move. If they jiggle like Jello and are triple the size they started at, that's when I call proof. Another good indicator of a proofed croissant is being able to see all the different layers start to separate from each other. This works especially well with flat cutouts of croissants as opposed to the classic rolled croissants.

Smaller buns will not take as long to proof as big loaves, and croissants take longer than brioche. It's difficult to give exact timelines for how long proofing should take because so many factors are involved. But as a very general guideline, if proofing at 80 degrees F, croissants should take about 2½ hours, a brioche loaf will take 1½ to 2 hours, and buns take roughly 1½ hours.

1 A properly proofed croissant will feel pillowy and aerated all the way through.

2 You can see the layers of this croissant cutout start to separate: that's a sure sign it's properly proofed.

BRIOCHE

Brioche is pure magic—ethereally light, impossibly buttery, and achingly soft. Of all the pastries on Earth, a well-executed brioche is my favorite to eat. Brioche is technically a bread, but it is so highly enriched with milk, eggs, and butter that it serves as a great base for pastry. In fact the famous phrase (falsely attributed to Marie Antoinette) "Let them eat cake" more literally translates from French to "Let them eat brioche."

Now, the world of brioche is a very wide and varied one. Since brioche has so many applications, from sandwich loaves to doughnuts to babka to burger buns, there are many formulas for making it, and each serves a different purpose. For example, if you want to make a brioche that will stand up to a stiff filling, such as a cinnamon roll, that formula may include less butter than one intended to make a loaf. The amount of fat in each formula dictates how soft and tender the brioche will be. Some of the recipes in this chapter may use a different dough recipe than the pillar brioche to better serve that product. But while the proportions of the dough ingredients may differ, the process of mixing them will be the same.

Let's dive into some brioche theory before attempting the pillar recipe. Brioche requires a long mixing time and specific temperatures. Make sure your butter is somewhat soft and pliable but not melty and all the rest of your ingredients are cold. Temperature is important because brioche dough is an emulsion: you are suspending the fat molecules in the dough much like when you make mayonnaise. If your dough is very hot when you add the butter, the fat will melt out and the resulting loaf will be at once greasy and dry. Because the brioche must mix for a long time before butter is added, and friction from the mixing process creates heat, it is important to start with cold ingredients. If you live in a hot environment, keep your flour in the freezer for 30 minutes before starting.

A Note on Doughnuts

I use a different dough recipe for doughnuts because it is slightly leaner (less fatty) and has a better texture when fried than the pillar brioche recipe. This dough requires an extra step of making a biga, which is a simple yeasted preferment (a portion of the dough that is fermented for several hours before mixing), that adds a lot of flavor to the final product. Other than making the biga, the process of mixing this dough is the exact same as in the Pillar Brioche recipe. Because the biga takes twelve hours to mature, you'll need to add an extra day to your timeline. So if you want doughnuts for Sunday brunch, make the biga Friday evening.

Develop Gluten

You'll want to create a somewhat strong network of protein strands to build the strength of the dough before adding fat. If you underdevelop the gluten, it will take too long to form a smooth dough after fat is added, and the dough might get too hot to hold the butter. This is because fat inhibits gluten formation. If you fully develop the gluten, meaning your dough ball completely comes off the sides of the bowl and looks smooth, it will be challenging to incorporate the butter at that point. So when we're mixing, we're going to take it somewhere in the middle. I want to see some gluten formation, which is indicated by the dough balling up around the hook as it mixes; it will start to come away from the sides of the bowl somewhat, but not all the way. It will not be smooth, but it will look stronger than when we first started mixing (photo 1, page 36).

Add Fat

Your butter, unlike your other ingredients, should be room temperature, soft and pliable but not melty (photo 2). This is because the butter will incorporate into your dough much faster if it is of a similar consistency. If you add cold, hard butter to a soft dough, the dough is going to have to work harder to break it down, and you risk overheating it. If your butter is as soft as your dough, they'll get along much better, and incorporating it will not take as long. You'll want to add the butter in three additions, letting it incorporate fully before adding more. This goes back to the idea of brioche being an emulsion; if you add all the fat at once, it won't be suspended in the dough properly and will likely melt out when you bake it.

Once all the butter is incorporated, your dough will look lighter and smoother (photo 3).

Perform the Windowpane Test

Lightly wet your hands and pinch off a golf ball–size portion of dough. Gently stretch it and hold it up to the light. If you can see through the dough like a windowpane, without it tearing, it has passed the test (photo 4). If it tears before it can get thin enough to see through, that's how you know the gluten isn't developed enough to take it off the mixer. Throw it back in the mixer and continue to mix until it passes this test.

Let It Ferment

While you certainly can try to shape freshly mixed brioche right away, it is so much easier to do when it is cold. I always mix my brioche the day before I want to shape and bake it. Not only is it easier to work with, but it also deepens the flavors by getting a long, slow, overnight fermentation. When you store brioche in the fridge overnight, make sure it is covered with plastic wrap, leaving enough room for it to grow in size. You can leave it in the fridge for up to 24 hours after it is mixed.

144 grams milk
160 grams eggs
(3 to 4 eggs,
see Note on
page 40)
7 grams yeast
400 grams flour, plus
more for dusting
50 grams sugar
9 grams salt
240 grams butter
Oil, for greasing
Nonstick cooking
spray, for greasing

For the egg wash
1 egg yolk
2 tablespoons heavy
cream or milk

PILLAR BRIOCHE

This brioche loaf is moderately enriched with butter and is a perfect canvas for a thick smear of jam or a sprinkling of cinnamon and sugar. It is one of those things that is greater than the sum of its parts, at once decadently rich and delightfully airy. It is sturdy enough to make a sandwich on and delicate enough to eat on its own.

Special equipment

9-by-4-by-4-inch loaf pan, proofing box

Timeline

DAY ONE mixing dough (30 to 45 minutes), fermenting dough (overnight)

DAY TWO shaping dough (15 minutes), proofing dough (1½ to 3 hours), baking brioche (50 to 60 minutes)

MIX THE DOUGH Place the milk, eggs, yeast, flour, sugar, and salt in the bowl of a stand mixer fitted with the hook attachment. Start the mixer on medium-low speed (speed 4 if you're using a KitchenAid) and let it come together.

Mix for about 18 minutes or until you see a ball forming around the dough hook and it has not quite pulled away from the sides and bottom of the bowl. Stop to scrape the dough down from the hook and the sides of the bowl a couple times during this process, if needed.

Keeping the mixer on medium-low speed, add about one-third of the butter. Wait for the butter to be fully incorporated into the dough before adding more. Then add another one-third of the butter, letting it fully incorporate before adding the last third.

continued

When all the butter is added, keep mixing until the dough looks smooth and glossy and pulls away from the sides of the bowl. Another bowl scraping may be necessary here. Once it's smooth and glossy, perform the windowpane test (see page 37).

Transfer the dough into a lightly oiled bowl (it should be at least double the size of the dough to allow for expansion), and place plastic wrap over the top of the bowl. Put it straight into the refrigerator to let it ferment and firm up overnight.

SHAPE AND ROLL OUT THE DOUGH To shape the brioche loaf, turn the dough out onto a lightly floured surface and gently press it to remove the air.

Using a rolling pin, roll the dough into a 9-by-14-inch flat rectangle with the 9-inch side closest to you. Occasionally lift the dough off the countertop to make sure it's not sticking. If it is sticking, throw a little more flour underneath it.

Once the rectangle is rolled out, start from the edge closest to you and roll it up into a cylinder. The ending cylinder should be the length of your pan. I prefer USA Pan's 9-by-4-by-4-inch loaf pan for its high, straight sides, but this is purely an aesthetic choice; a standard loaf pan will work just fine. Generously grease the pan with nonstick cooking spray and place the cylinder in it, pressing down gently to fill out the bottom of the pan.

PROOF THE DOUGH Place the pan in your proofing box or use the proofing method of your choice. Proof the dough as described on page 26.

BAKE THE DOUGH Preheat the oven to 350 degrees F.

Just before baking, egg wash according to the instructions on page 23. Pop the loaf in the middle rack of the oven and bake for 50 to 60 minutes or until it has a golden-brown crust and the internal temperature is 200 degrees F. If the top is getting too dark before it's done, lightly tent it with aluminum foil to prevent burning. Let it rest in its pan for 5 minutes before carefully unmolding it onto a wire cooling rack. This loaf is best the day it is made but will keep tightly wrapped at room temperature for up to 3 days.

NOTE If your eggs do not come out to an even 160 grams, get as close to that number as you can without going over, then make up the difference with milk. Eggs usually weigh right around 50 grams each.

For the French toast

1 recipe Pillar Brioche (page 39), preferably day-old

6 eggs

270 grams whole milk

4 garlic cloves, finely chopped

2½ teaspoons salt

½ teaspoon freshly ground black pepper

2 scallions, roughly chopped

4 to 6 tablespoons butter

225 grams grated hard cheese, such as Asiago, Parmesan and/or pecorino Romano

For the chive cream cheese

225 grams cream cheese, at room temperature

20 grams finely sliced chives

½ teaspoon salt

¼ teaspoon freshly ground black pepper

For the crispy shallot topping

3 tablespoons neutral oil, such as avocado, plus more as needed

1 shallot, thinly sliced

¼ teaspoon salt

Cheese-Crusted Scallion French Toast

with Savory Whipped Cream Cheese

Hosting brunch should be a relaxing endeavor, yet savory options that don't require cooking to order are few and far between. This is a unique savory main for brunch, like if a bagel with schmear had a love child with French toast. It's cheesy, custardy, crunchy, and full of oniony goodness. And the best part is that you can make it ahead of time, which gives you more time to sip mimosas with your guests!

Special equipment

Immersion blender

Timeline

DAY ONE preparing slices (3 hours to overnight), soaking in custard (1 hour)

DAY TWO making chive cream cheese (5 minutes), cooking and serving French toast (20 to 30 minutes), making crispy shallot topping (15 to 20 minutes)

MAKE THE FRENCH TOAST Slice the brioche loaf by trimming off the two ends, then cutting the rest of the loaf into six even slices, about 1¼ inches thick. Arrange on a baking sheet and let them get stale.

In a medium bowl, combine the eggs, milk, garlic, salt, pepper, and scallions with an immersion blender until smooth. Pour evenly over the brioche slices, wrap the baking sheet in plastic, and refrigerate for at least 1 hour, up to overnight. Turn them over halfway through soaking so they absorb the custard evenly on both sides.

MAKE THE CHIVE CREAM CHEESE Right before cooking the French toast, place the cream cheese, chives, salt, and pepper in a stand mixer with the paddle attachment. Whip on medium-high speed until combined and a little aerated and spreadable. Set aside.

Preheat the oven to 200 degrees F.

In a large nonstick skillet on the stove over medium heat, melt 2 tablespoons butter. Carefully dip each slice of soaked brioche in the grated cheese to evenly coat both sides. Fry the brioche slice in the skillet until deeply browned and cooked through, 4 to 5 minutes per side. Lower the heat if the cheese gets too dark before the center is set. Put on a baking sheet and place in the oven to keep warm while you repeat with the remaining slices. Add another 2 tablespoons butter with each round of cooking or if the pan ever looks dry.

MEANWHILE, MAKE THE CRISPY SHALLOT TOPPING Put the oil and shallot in a small saucepan. The oil should just cover the shallot; add more oil if needed. Heat over medium, stirring occasionally, until the shallot turns a light-golden color. Let it drain on a paper towel-lined plate and season with the salt as soon as it comes off the heat. Set aside.

Serve the French toast hot with a generous dollop of the chive cream cheese and a pile of crispy shallot topping.

1 recipe Pillar
  Brioche (page 39),
  preferably day-old
4 to 6 tablespoons
  fat

Pan-Fried Brioche

for Canapés Three Ways

Everyone needs a great hors d'oeuvre recipe up their sleeve for
that girls' night in or the fanciest Super Bowl party anyone's
ever been to. For all three of these recipes, you'll want to begin
by baking a loaf of the pillar brioche and letting it cool completely. Then choose one (or all) of the variations to complete
the canapés—use the type of fat that calls to you for frying!

Timeline

DAY ONE making brioche (5 hours plus overnight fermentation), slicing
and drying out brioche (10 minutes)

DAY TWO making canapés (30 to 45 minutes)

Trim off the crusts and slice the brioche into 4-inch-long, 1-inch-wide,
and 1-inch-deep batons. It will be easier to slice if it's day-old and a
little stale.

Get a large nonstick skillet over a medium heat to fry the brioche
batons. Heat whichever fat you're using until shimmering (if using
butter, wait until it stops foaming). Carefully place about half of the
batons in the pan, being careful not to overcrowd.

Turn the heat down to medium and fry for 30 seconds to 1 minute per
side, lowering the heat if the brioche is getting too dark. You're looking
for a golden-brown color on all sides. Turn them over as many times
as you need to achieve the color you want. Let them drain on a paper
towel–lined plate and repeat with the remaining batons. Let cool
before topping.

continued

Duck Fat–Fried Brioche Canapés

with Apricot and Cherry Mostarda

Makes 15 to 20 canapés

For the mostarda

150 grams dried apricots, diced

115 grams dried cherries

120 grams dry white wine

1 small shallot, finely diced

40 grams white wine vinegar

25 grams butter

15 grams Dijon mustard

5 grams dry mustard

1 recipe Pan-Fried Brioche (page 45), using duck fat

MAKE THE MOSTARDA In a small sauce pot, bring the apricots, cherries, wine, shallot, 40 grams of water, and the vinegar to a boil. Cover it, reduce the heat to a simmer, and let cook, stirring occasionally, until the fruit absorbs almost all of the liquid. Take it off the heat; stir in the butter, Dijon, and dry mustard; and let cool to room temperature before using. This may make more than you'll need, but it will keep in the fridge for at least 1 month and is delicious with all sorts of roasted meats.

Follow the recipe for Pan-Fried Brioche using duck fat.

Spoon about 2 teaspoons of the mostarda onto each brioche baton in a decorative way. Arrange on a platter and serve.

Butter-Fried Brioche Canapés

with Crème Fraîche and Caviar

Makes 15 to 20 canapés

1 recipe Pan-Fried Brioche (page 45), using butter

3 ounces crème fraîche

1 tin caviar

Chives, cut into 1½-inch segments, for garnishing

Follow the recipe for Pan-Fried Brioche using butter.

Spoon a dollop of crème fraîche onto each baton and create a small well in the center of the dollop. Spoon caviar into the well, and garnish with a chive segment. Arrange on a platter and serve.

**Makes 15 to
20 canapés**

1 recipe Pan-Fried
  Brioche (page 45),
  using olive oil
4 ounces mascarpone
Salt and freshly ground
  black pepper
4 ounces peach
  preserves, such as
  Bonne Maman
8 to 10 slices
  prosciutto, torn into
  thin strips
Microgreens, for
  garnishing
  (see Note)

Olive Oil–Fried Brioche Canapés
with Mascarpone, Peach, and Prosciutto

Follow the recipe for Pan-Fried Brioche using olive oil.

In a small bowl, season the mascarpone with salt and pepper to taste. Spoon a dollop of mascarpone onto each baton and create a small well in the center of the dollop. Fill the well with peach preserves, then top with thin ribbons of prosciutto and garnish with microgreens. Arrange on a platter and serve.

NOTE If you can get micro basil, I highly recommend using this as your microgreen for extra flavor.

Makes 2 large loaves

For the dough
480 grams flour,
  plus more for
  dusting
190 grams eggs
  (3 to 4 eggs)
115 grams whole milk
75 grams sugar
75 grams water
8 grams yeast
12 grams salt
120 grams butter, at
  room temperature

For the filling
110 grams butter,
  melted
105 grams gochujang
30 grams flour
12 grams brown sugar
50 grams egg
  (about 1 egg)

For the egg wash
1 egg yolk
2 tablespoons heavy
  cream or milk

Gochujang Babka

I'm going to let you in on one of my many hot takes in the pastry world: chocolate babka is overrated. I love the *idea* of chocolate babka but always find its execution to be lacking. The brioche is dry on the outside; the chocolate has become chalky and brittle in the oven. No thank you! This is my answer to babka: savory, spicy, and supremely buttery loaves that are endlessly snackable.

This is one of the brioche recipes that calls for a different dough. Mixing will be the same as the pillar brioche recipe, but the dough will be quite a bit softer.

Special equipment

Two 9-by-4-by-4-inch loaf pans

Timeline

DAY ONE mixing dough (30 to 45 minutes), fermenting dough (overnight)

DAY TWO making filling (5 minutes), shaping dough (10 to 15 minutes), proofing dough (1½ to 2 hours), baking babka (35 to 40 minutes)

MAKE THE DOUGH Following the steps in the recipe for Pillar Brioche (page 39), mix the flour, eggs, milk, sugar, 75 grams of water, the yeast, and salt for the dough. Then add the butter. Refrigerate overnight in a lightly oiled bowl covered in plastic wrap.

MAKE THE FILLING Whisk the butter, gochujang, flour, and brown sugar together; it will look lumpy and broken. Whisk in the egg; it should magically emulsify into a smooth paste. Set aside.

Generously flour a surface and turn the dough out onto it. Generously flour the top of the dough as well. Using a rolling pin, roll the dough out into a 15-by-24-inch rectangle, with the 15-inch sides at the top and bottom and the 24-inch sides to the left and right. Periodically lift the dough off the countertop to make sure it isn't sticking. If you find that it is sticking, add a little more flour underneath it.

continued

SPREAD FILLING Once you have the dough rolled out, spread the filling evenly across the entire surface of the dough (photo 1). Go right up to all the edges except the one farthest from you; you'll want to leave about a ½ inch of space along that far edge to create a seam when you roll it up.

ROLL Starting at the bottom edge, roll up the dough in a spiral, like a cinnamon roll (photo 2). Keep going all the way until you've rolled it all up, ending at the filling–less edge. Transfer the log onto a baking sheet and toss it in the freezer for 10 to 15 minutes to firm up.

Prepare two 9-by-4-by-4-inch loaf pans by greasing them generously with pan spray. If you're not confident in their nonstickiness, you can line the bottoms with parchment paper and grease those as well.

TWIST Take the babka log out of the freezer and place it on the counter. Now take a sharp knife and slice the log lengthwise to create two long strands. Cut each of these in half crosswise to end up with four shorter strands. Each loaf will consist of two strands. With the cut side facing up, twist two of the strands together, then place in the prepared loaf pan (photo 3). Repeat with the remaining two strands.

Proof the dough as described on page 26.

Just before baking, egg wash according to instructions on page 23. Bake in the center of the oven at 350 degrees F for 35 to 40 minutes or until the center of the loaf is 200 degrees F. If the tops are getting too dark before they're done, lightly tent with aluminum foil. Let cool in the pans for 5 to 10 minutes before upending them onto a cooling rack. Enjoy at room temperature. These loaves keep well wrapped in plastic at room temperature for up to 3 days.

**Makes 12 to
15 doughnuts**

For the biga
105 grams flour
57 grams water
Small pinch of yeast

For the brioche dough
588 grams flour, plus
  more for dusting
190 grams eggs (3 to
  4 eggs)
190 grams milk
60 grams sugar
34 grams brown
  sugar
16 grams yeast
14 grams salt
150 grams butter

*For the vanilla
pastry cream*
820 grams milk
196 grams sugar,
  divided
1 vanilla bean, split
  in half lengthwise,
  seeds scraped
112 grams egg yolks
38 grams cornstarch
90 grams butter,
  cubed
2 quarts vegetable oil
1 cup sugar

Crème Brûlée Doughnut

I must admit that I rarely order dessert when I go out to eat, but one dessert I will order any time I see it on a menu is crème brûlée. There's something about the rich vanilla custard and crunchy caramel that just rings all my bells. I'm usually a purist when it comes to this dessert, but it translates very well to doughnuts. I promise you will not have any leftovers of these. Spring for a real vanilla bean when making the custard, as its flavor will far outshine extract.

I use a different dough recipe for doughnuts because it is slightly leaner (less fatty) and has a better texture when fried than the pillar brioche recipe. This dough requires an extra step of making a biga, which is a simple yeasted preferment (a portion of the dough that is fermented for several hours before mixing) that adds a lot of flavor to the final product. Other than making the biga, the process of mixing this dough is the exact same as in the Pillar Brioche recipe. Because the biga takes twelve hours to mature, you'll need to add an extra day to your timeline. So if you want doughnuts for Sunday brunch, make the biga Friday evening.

Timeline

DAY ONE mixing biga (5 minutes), fermenting biga (12 to 16 hours)

DAY TWO mixing dough (30 minutes), prepping pastry cream (20 minutes), fermenting dough (overnight)

DAY THREE shaping doughnuts (5 minutes), proofing doughnuts (1½ to 2 hours), frying doughnuts (20 to 30 minutes), filling doughnuts (5 minutes), making caramel (10 minutes), dipping doughnuts (15 minutes)

continued

MAKE THE BIGA Two days before you want to eat the doughnuts, mix the flour, 57 grams of water, and the yeast together until homogenous. Let it sit to ferment in a covered bowl at room temperature for 12 to 16 hours.

MAKE THE BRIOCHE DOUGH Place the flour, eggs, milk, both sugars, yeast, and salt in the bowl of a stand mixer fitted with the hook attachment. Add the mature biga. Mix the brioche dough following the steps in the Pillar Brioche recipe (page 39). Add the butter after the gluten has developed a bit. Refrigerate overnight in a lightly oiled bowl covered with plastic wrap.

MAKE THE VANILLA PASTRY CREAM In a small saucepot, heat the milk, 98 grams of the sugar, and the vanilla seeds over medium heat. In a medium heatproof bowl, combine the yolks, cornstarch, and remaining 98 grams of the sugar and whisk thoroughly. When the milk comes to a boil, temper it into the yolk mixture: Add a small amount of hot liquid and whisk quickly to combine. Add a little more, whisking constantly, until about two-thirds of the hot liquid are added to the yolks. Pour the yolk mixture back into the pot and continue to cook over medium heat, whisking constantly, until thickened, anywhere between 30 seconds and 2 minutes, depending on your heat level. Cook for 30 seconds longer after it thickens to cook out the cornstarch taste. Take it off the heat and whisk in the butter until homogenous. Transfer to a shallow container and place plastic wrap on the surface to prevent a skin from forming. Refrigerate overnight.

Prepare some parchment paper by cutting twelve 4-inch squares; set aside. Lightly flour the counter and turn the dough out onto it. Roll the dough into a 12-by-16-inch rectangle of about ¼-inch thickness throughout. Use a 3-inch cookie cutter to cut out circles of dough. Place each circle of dough onto a square of parchment paper and put that on a baking sheet.

Proof the doughnuts as described on page 26. You do not need to egg wash these.

Fry the doughnuts in vegetable oil as described on page 60. Let cool to room temperature before filling.

Fill the doughnuts with pastry cream as described on page 24.

In a small, shallow saucepan, heat the sugar over high heat without disturbing until the edges begin to liquefy. Slowly and gently begin to stir the sugar until it all becomes liquid and takes on a deep amber color. Once the caramel is dark, take it off the heat immediately, but keep the burner on low. Set the saucepan on an oven mitt or trivet and *very carefully* dip the doughnuts into the caramel one at a time, letting any excess drip off the doughnut before turning it upright.

This process can be perilous; if you get caramel on you, quickly set the doughnut down and run your hand under cold water to prevent blisters. You can also wear latex gloves to do this, and if caramel gets on those, pull them off immediately to prevent a burn. I only warn you from experience, not to scare you! If the caramel starts to get too cold and you're creating little strands of spun sugar, put it back on the burner over low heat and stir until it's liquidy again. Then take back off the heat and continue.

Once all the doughnuts are dipped, pour the excess caramel onto a piece of parchment paper and let the saucepan soak in hot water. Once the caramel hardens on the paper, you can toss it out. Enjoy the doughnuts within a few hours.

Nduja Doughnut

Makes 12 to 15 doughnuts

For the biga
105 grams flour
57 grams of water
Small pinch of yeast

For the brioche dough
588 grams flour, plus
  more for dusting
190 grams eggs (3 to
  4 eggs)
190 grams milk
60 grams sugar
34 grams brown sugar
16 grams yeast
14 grams salt
150 grams butter

For the roasted garlic
1 head of garlic
2 tablespoons olive oil
Salt

For the panko coating
1 cup panko bread
  crumbs
2 tablespoons Italian
  seasoning

For the nduja filling
250 grams high-
  quality full-fat ricotta
  cheese
15 grams roasted garlic
170 grams nduja
  sausage, at room
  temperature
  (see Note on
  page 59)
20 grams olive oil
Salt and freshly ground
  black pepper
2 quarts vegetable oil
Pickled piparra
  peppers, such as
  Matiz brand, for
  garnishing

We always include a savory doughnut in our seasonal menus at the bakery. This pizza-inspired recipe came from one of my pastry cooks who had a passion for pushing boundaries in the food world. Nduja is a spiced, spreadable salami often used in pasta or pizza dishes. Mixed with ricotta and roasted garlic, it makes for a unique and ultra-savory doughnut filling. It's something we kept on the menu even after he left because it's so interesting and delicious!

This dough has less fat than the pillar brioche recipe and requires an extra step of making a biga (for more on this, see A Note on Doughnuts on page 34.) Otherwise, the process is exactly the same as in the pillar recipe.

Special equipment

Wok or large skillet for deep-frying, mesh draining rack, piping bag, 3- inch circle cookie cutter, instant-read thermometer, heatproof slotted spoon, chopsticks (optional), kitchen timer, food processor, spray bottle (optional), toothpicks

Timeline

DAY ONE mixing biga (5 minutes), fermenting biga (12 to 16 hours)

DAY TWO mixing dough (30 to 45 minutes), fermenting dough (overnight), roasting garlic (1 hour)

DAY THREE shaping doughnuts (5 minutes), proofing doughnuts (1½ to 2 hours), prepping filling (5 minutes), frying doughnuts (20 to 30 minutes), filling doughnuts (5 minutes)

MAKE THE BIGA Two days before you want to eat the doughnuts, mix the flour, 57 grams of water, and the yeast together until homogenous. Let it sit to ferment in a lightly oiled covered bowl at room temperature for 12 to 16 hours.

continued

Nduja Doughnut, continued

MAKE THE BRIOCHE DOUGH Place the flour, eggs, milk, both sugars, yeast, and salt in the bowl of a stand mixer fitted with the hook attachment. Add the mature biga. Mix the brioche dough following the steps in the Pillar Brioche recipe (page 39). Add the butter after the gluten has developed a bit. Refrigerate overnight in a lightly oiled bowl covered with plastic wrap.

MAKE THE ROASTED GARLIC Preheat the oven to 400 degrees F.

Cut the top off of the garlic head to expose the cloves. Place on a square of aluminum foil and pour the olive oil over the cloves. Season with salt. Wrap the head in aluminum foil, place on a baking sheet or small ovenproof skillet, and bake for about 1 hour or until the cloves deepen in color and become spreadable. Once they cool, pop the cloves out into a bowl and mash them into a paste. This makes more than you'll need for the doughnuts, but it's great on everything from toast to potatoes to roasted meats, so it won't go to waste. I promise! Reserve 15 grams of the roasted garlic for the doughnuts and keep the extra in a covered container in the fridge for up to 1 month.

MAKE THE PANKO COATING Combine panko and Italian seasoning in a wide, shallow bowl or a pie dish and set aside.

Prepare some parchment paper by cutting twelve 4-inch squares; set aside. Lightly flour the counter and turn the dough out onto it. Roll the dough into a 12-by-16-inch rectangle of about ¼-inch thickness throughout. Use a 3-inch cookie cutter to cut out circles of dough. Gently wet both sides of each doughnut; I use a spray bottle of water to get the doughnuts damp, but you can also brush a small amount of water on each side with a pastry brush. Then toss the doughnuts in the bowl of seasoned panko to coat. Place each circle of dough onto a square of parchment paper and put that on a baking sheet.

Proof the doughnuts as described on page 26. You do not need to egg wash these.

WHILE THEY PROOF, MAKE THE NDUJA FILLING Process the ricotta and roasted garlic in a food processor until smooth. Transfer to a medium bowl and add the nduja and olive oil. Stir to combine into a smooth paste, returning to the food processor if needed. Season with salt and pepper. Transfer to a piping bag and set aside.

Fry the doughnuts in vegetable oil as described on page 60.

Once the doughnuts are cool, fill them using the method described on page 24. Skewer a piparra pepper with a toothpick and spear each doughnut with one. Serve immediately.

NOTE Nduja varies quite a bit from brand to brand. Choose a smoother one, since that will be easier to pipe, and make sure to taste the filling before adding salt, as some ndujas are much saltier than others. My preferred brand is Tempesta.

Frying Doughnuts

I like to use a wok when deep-frying at home, but a large shallow pan will work as well. Heat 2 quarts of neutral oil over high heat to 350 degrees F. While you're waiting for the oil to heat up, set up a baking sheet with a wire mesh draining rack on it and get a slotted spoon, kitchen timer, and chopsticks (optional but helpful!). The biggest challenge with deep-frying at home is keeping the oil at a constant temperature. Once the oil reaches 350 degrees F, lower the heat to maintain the temperature. Don't fry right away; instead, spend some time calibrating the heat to keep the oil at 350 degrees F. When you add dough to it, the temperature of the oil will drop, so play around with a scrap piece of dough to test it before committing to an actual doughnut.

Once you're comfortable with the oil temperature and how to manipulate it on your stove, using both hands, carefully lower a square of parchment paper with a doughnut on it into the oil and start the timer. Keep hold of one corner of the parchment paper the doughnut is on; once the oil hits the underside of the doughnut, the parchment paper should slip right out. You do have to get your hand quite close to the oil, but as long as you are gentle and don't splash the oil at all, it should be safe (see photo). Repeat with as many doughnuts as will fit in the pan without crowding (I got four doughnuts in my 12-inch wok at a time). Keep an eye on the oil temp and try to keep it as close to 350 degrees F as you can. Cook on one side for 2 minutes, then flip them over and cook for another 2 minutes.

When you flip a doughnut, always flip it away from you so if you accidentally splash oil, it will splash onto your stove and not you. I use chopsticks to flip doughnuts, but you can also use a metal fork or spoon. I push one side down with one chopstick and then lift the other side up with the other chopstick, and that flips it over with minimal splashing. After you've cooked each side for 2 minutes, use the slotted spoon to transfer the doughnuts to the mesh rack and let cool while you fry the others.

Makes 12 buns

1 recipe Pillar Brioche (page 39)
200 grams dark chocolate, finely chopped, or semisweet mini chocolate chips
Oil, for greasing
Butter, at room temperature, for greasing
Coarse demerara sugar, for coating
Flour, for dusting

For the caramel chantilly
500 grams heavy cream, divided
100 grams sugar

For the egg wash
1 egg yolk
2 tablespoons heavy cream or milk

Chocolate-Chunk Brioche Buns

with Caramel Chantilly

There are few examples of a more classic pairing than chocolate and caramel, but usually when I picture that flavor profile, it comes as something dense and rich, like chocolate-coated caramels or caramel-swirl brownies or something to do with ice cream. All of which are great—don't get me wrong! This recipe, however, flips that idea on its head and makes an incredibly light and fluffy chocolate caramel dessert. The buttery, airy brioche is studded with chunks of dark chocolate, then filled with an almost-bitter, slightly sweet, whipped caramel chantilly cream. It feels decadent without weighing you down.

Special equipment

Immersion blender, brioche à tête molds (see Note on page 64) or muffin tin, piping bag with star tip

Timeline

DAY ONE mixing dough (30 to 45 minutes), fermenting dough (overnight), making caramel chantilly (20 minutes)

DAY TWO shaping dough (15 to 20 minutes), proofing dough (1½ to 2 hours), baking buns (25 to 30 minutes), filling buns (10 minutes)

Prepare the recipe for Pillar Brioche but add the chopped chocolate at the very end of the mixing process, after the butter has been incorporated and gluten has been developed. Mix on low speed just until the chocolate is evenly distributed throughout the dough. Refrigerate overnight in a lightly oiled bowl covered with plastic wrap.

MAKE THE CARAMEL CHANTILLY In a small saucepan, heat 100 grams of the cream over medium high heat until steaming and set aside. Put the sugar in another thick-bottomed saucepan over high heat. Let the sugar melt without disturbing it. Once the edges start to melt, gently stir the sugar until it caramelizes. Once it has reached a deep amber color, add the hot cream in several additions. Be careful here, as it will

continued

bubble up a lot! Once the cream is added, take it off the heat and pour it into a heatproof bowl. Nestle an immersion blender into the hot caramel and turn it on low speed, being careful not to let it splash or sputter. Pour the remaining 400 grams of cream into the caramel in a steady stream while the blender runs. Once all the cream is incorporated, wrap in plastic and refrigerate overnight.

The next day, prep the brioche molds or muffin tin. Coat the inside of each cavity with butter, smearing it evenly with your hands so there's a thin film covering the surface (photo 1). Fill the cavity with the demerara sugar and then pour it out (photo 2). You should have a baking vessel that's completely coated in butter and sugar.

Turn the dough out onto a floured surface and divide it into twelve equal portions, 90 to 100 grams each. Roll the dough portions into balls, creating tension in the dough. If a chocolate piece tears through to the outside, just pluck it from the edge and put it underneath the bun. You don't want any large chunks of chocolate on the surface of the bun as they'll burn in the oven.

Place each bun into a prepared mold. Proof the dough as described on page 26.

Just before baking, egg wash according to instructions on page 23. Bake in the oven at 350 degrees F for 25 minutes. Let cool for 5 minutes before carefully unmolding them from their baking vessels. If they stick at all, use a small offset spatula or paring knife to release them from the mold. Let cool completely on a wire rack.

Once cool, cut a triangle out of the top of each bun and reserve. Use a spoon to scoop out some of the center of the bun, creating a well for the chantilly. Whip the chantilly in a stand mixer fitted with the whisk attachment until stiff peaks form. Transfer to a piping bag fitted with a star tip and fill each bun, going up above the top of it as shown in the photo on page 62. Top each dollop of chantilly with the reserved triangle cutouts. Serve immediately.

If you do not plan to serve all of them on the same day, you can wrap unfilled brioche buns in plastic and keep them at room temperature for up to 2 days. Unused caramel chantilly can be kept covered in the refrigerator for up to 2 days but may need to be rewhipped before using again. Refresh the buns in the oven at 350 degrees F for 5 minutes, let cool slightly, and fill before eating.

NOTE You can find brioche à tête molds at specialty baking shops or at BakeDeco.com.

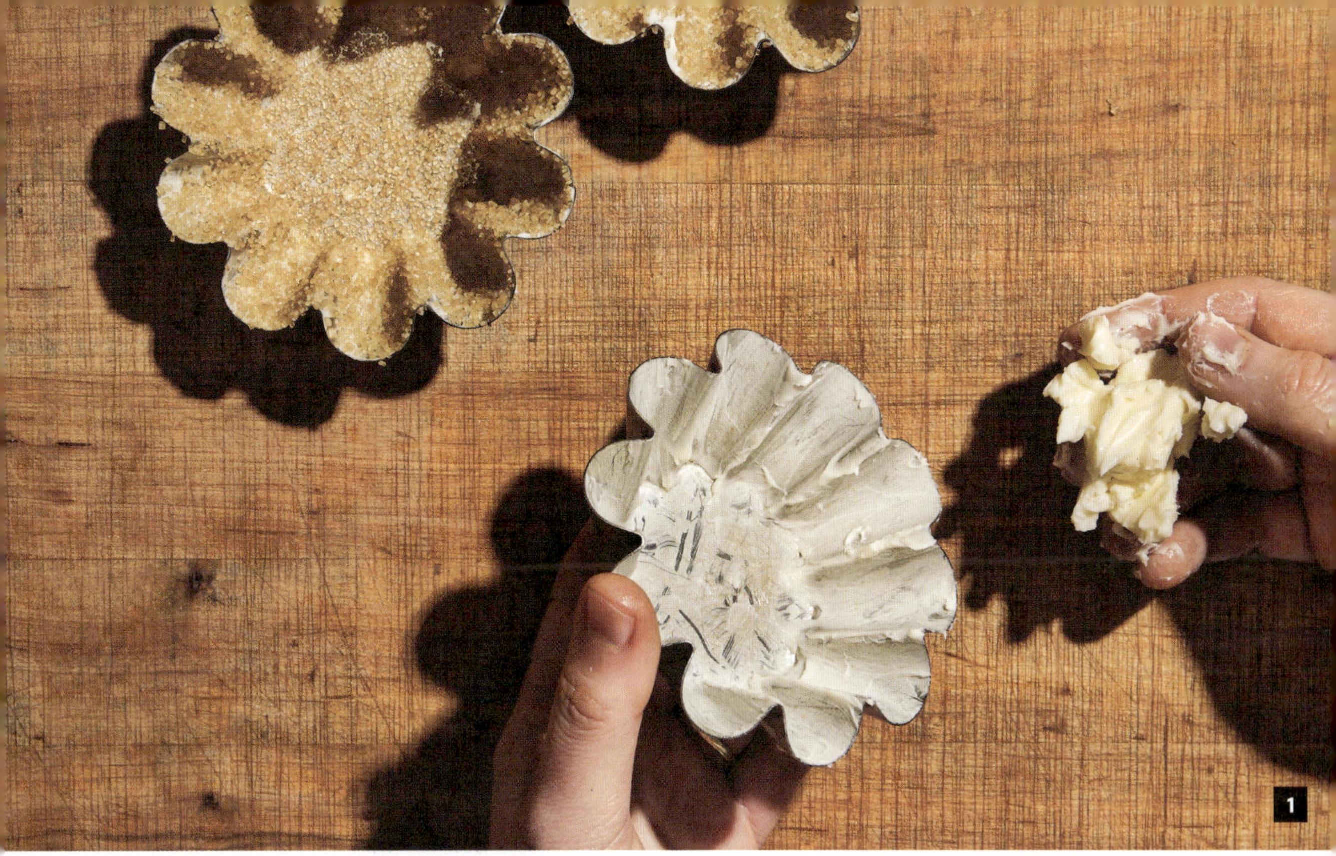
1

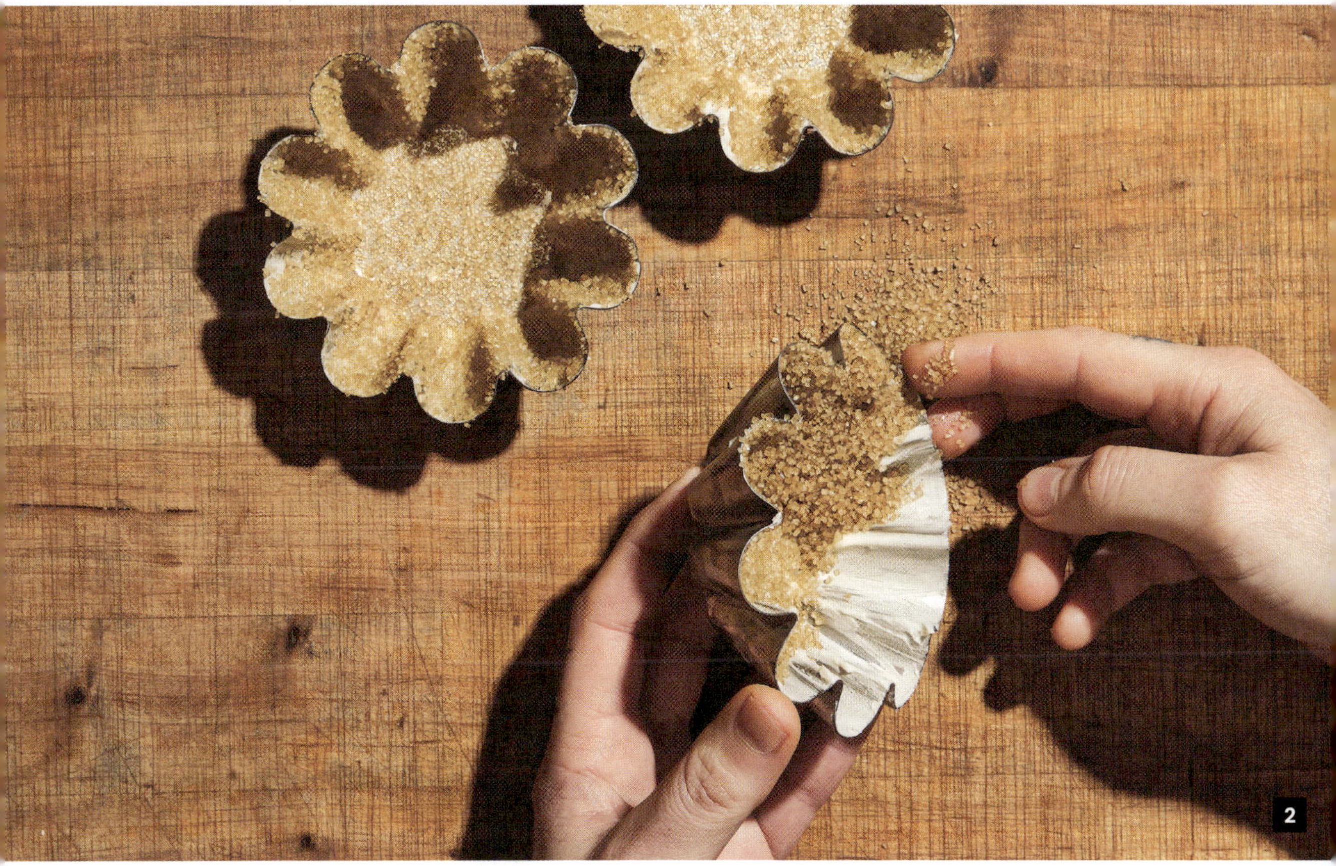
2

For the dough
1 recipe Pillar Brioche
   (page 39)
Flour, for dusting

For the passionfruit mousse
3 grams sheet gelatin
   (see page 10)
Ice water, for
   blooming
108 grams high-
   quality white
   chocolate, such as
   Valrhona
400 grams heavy
   cream, divided
120 grams
   passionfruit puree

For the coconut glaze
50 grams shredded
   coconut
250 grams high-
   quality white
   chocolate, such as
   Valrhona
40 grams coconut oil
1 lime

For the egg wash
1 egg yolk
2 tablespoons heavy
   cream or milk

Coconut-Glazed Passionfruit Maritozzi

I first encountered maritozzi when I went to Italy for a friend's wedding. There was a shop within walking distance of my apartment in Rome, a super old-school bakery manned by one flour-covered baker with huge forearms and a surly old lady who begrudgingly took my order. I sat in the punishing sun and devoured it. It was so simple, yet so good: a long, soft brioche bun filled with a swoop of whipped cream. That was it. I was immediately obsessed with making them. I've added a refreshing tropical twist to this version, something I wished was added to the one I had in the hot summer Roman sun.

Special equipment

Immersion blender, small offset spatula, piping bag

Timeline

DAY ONE mixing dough (30 to 45 minutes), making passionfruit mousse (15 minutes), making coconut glaze (10 minutes), fermenting dough (overnight)

DAY TWO shaping dough (10 to 15 minutes), proofing dough (1½ to 2 hours), baking buns (20 to 30 minutes), assembling maritozzi (30 minutes)

Make the brioche dough. Refrigerate overnight.

MAKE THE PASSIONFRUIT MOUSSE Bloom the gelatin by submerging it in ice water until softened. Squeeze excess water from the gelatin and place it in a small heatproof bowl with the white chocolate. Heat 200 grams of the cream in a small pot until boiling. Pour the hot cream over the chocolate and gelatin, and stir to melt and create a ganache. Use an immersion blender to make a smooth liquid. With the immersion blender running, stream in the remaining 200 grams of cream, then stream in the passionfruit puree, and mix until homogenous. Transfer to a container, cover with plastic wrap, and refrigerate overnight.

continued

*Coconut-Glazed
Passionfruit Maritozzi,
continued*

MAKE THE COCONUT GLAZE Preheat the oven to 350 degrees F.

Spread the shredded coconut out in a thin layer on a baking sheet and bake for 8 minutes or until toasted, stirring halfway through.

In a microwave-safe bowl, microwave the white chocolate and coconut oil in 30-second increments, stirring between each increment, until fully melted. Stir in the toasted coconut. Cover and leave at room temperature.

DIVIDE AND SHAPE THE DOUGH Turn the dough out onto a lightly floured surface and gently press it into a flat rectangle. Cut the dough into twelve equal portions, roughly 90 to 100 grams each, and roll each piece into a round ball. Place the balls onto a parchment-lined baking sheet, evenly spaced apart.

PROOF AND BAKE Proof the dough as described on page 26.

Just before baking, egg wash according to instructions on page 23. Bake the buns in the center of the oven at 350 degrees F for 20 minutes or until they have taken on a golden-brown color and are 200 degrees F internally. Let cool completely on a wire rack.

Once the buns are cool, whip the passionfruit mousse in a stand mixer fitted with the whisk attachment until medium stiff peaks form. Put the mousse in a piping bag and set aside.

ASSEMBLE THE BUNS With the "foot" of the bun on the counter, make a cut in the top of each bun, perpendicular to the counter, going almost all the way through the entire bun. Gently separate the two halves from each other, keeping the bottom "hinge" intact, to create an opening about 1½ inches wide. Cut a small opening in the piping bag filled with mousse, and fill each bun with the mousse (photo 1). Use a small offset spatula or butter knife to smooth the mousse out (photo 2). It should be flush with the edge of the brioche. Place the buns in the freezer for 20 minutes to firm up.

Meanwhile, microwave the coconut glaze in 20-second increments, stirring between each increment, until juuuuuuuust melted. If the glaze gets too hot, it's going to look very thin on the pastry, so you want it to be just barely melted and thus more viscous. Take the buns out of the freezer and, one by one, dip each bun in the glaze, covering half of the bun. Place the buns back on the baking sheet to let the glaze set. Using a Microplane, zest the lime over the top of the buns. Serve immediately.

If you do not plan to serve all of them on the same day, you can wrap unfilled brioche buns in plastic and keep them at room temperature for up to 2 days. Unused passionfruit mousse can be kept covered in the refrigerator for up to 2 days but may need to be rewhipped before using again. Unused coconut glaze can stay covered at room temperature for up to 1 week. Refresh the buns in the oven at 350 degrees F for 5 minutes, let cool slightly, and fill before eating.

NOTE You can find passionfruit puree at specialty baking stores or online. Look for purees that are made from just fruit and sugar, with no other additives. A high-quality puree usually contains about 10 percent sugar.

For the dough
½ recipe Pillar
   Brioche (page
   39, see Note on
   page 75)
Flour, for dusting

*For the raspberry
whipped ganache*
2 grams sheet gelatin
Ice water, for
   blooming
150 grams high-
   quality white
   chocolate
200 grams heavy
   cream
70 grams raspberry
   puree (see Note on
   page 72)

*For the raspberry
syrup*
50 grams sugar
50 grams water
50 grams raspberry
   puree

For the egg wash
1 egg yolk

For assembly
2 tablespoons heavy
   cream or milk
Pearl sugar, for
   topping
1 recipe Black
   Sesame Mousseline
   (recipe follows)
One pint fresh
   raspberries
Powdered sugar,
   for dusting

Raspberry Tropézienne
with Black Sesame Mousseline

I've heard rumors there are people out there who don't like cake. Go ahead, clutch your pearls, but it's true! Maybe you are such a person; just know this is a safe space for you and I'm not judging by any means. Heck, there is a lot of *bad* cake out there. So let's say you know someone who's one of these people, and they have a birthday coming up. What do you do now? You make them a tarte Tropézienne.

This recipe is not for the faint of heart, but all the planning and work will be so worthwhile. The brioche is soft and tender with a slight crisp to it from the pearl sugar. The raspberry syrup adds moisture and a touch of acidity to the brioche base. Inside, raspberry whipped ganache is lighter than air and bursting with berry flavor, while the black sesame mousseline is a dense, creamy, nutty accent to make this seem richer than just a brioche with whipped cream. Fresh raspberries interspersed throughout will add a pop of color and texture to each bite.

Special equipment

9-inch cake pan, food processor, immersion blender, two piping bags, two plain piping tips

Timeline

DAY ONE prepping black sesame mousseline (1 hour), mixing dough (30 to 45 minutes), prepping raspberry whipped ganache (15 minutes), prepping raspberry syrup (5 minutes), fermenting dough (overnight)

DAY TWO shaping dough (10 minutes), proofing dough (1½ to 2½ hours), baking brioche (22 to 25 minutes), assembling Tropézienne (30 to 45 minutes)

continued

Mix a half batch of Pillar Brioche.

MAKE THE RASPBERRY WHIPPED GANACHE Bloom the gelatin by soaking it in ice water until it softens, then squeeze excess water from it and put it in a small heatproof bowl with the white chocolate. Bring the cream to a boil, pour it over the white chocolate and gelatin, and let sit for 1 minute before stirring to combine. Use the immersion blender to make a homogenous mixture. Pour in the raspberry puree and blend again until completely homogenous. Pour into a container, cover in plastic wrap to prevent a skin from forming, and refrigerate overnight.

NOTE You can buy raspberry puree online, such as Boiron brand.

MAKE THE RASPBERRY SYRUP Combine the sugar, 50 grams water, and the raspberry puree in a small saucepan. Bring to a simmer over medium-high heat, stirring to completely dissolve the sugar. Transfer to a container and refrigerate overnight.

Prepare a 9-inch cake pan by greasing the sides and bottom with pan spray. If you're not confident of its nonstickiness, you can put a round of parchment paper on the bottom and spray that down with cooking oil too. Take the brioche dough out of the fridge and turn it out onto a lightly floured surface. Dust the top with flour as well. Gently roll or press the dough into a 9-inch disc, making sure it is of even thickness throughout. It doesn't have to be a perfect circle, but it should be close to the size of your cake pan. Lift it up and place it into the prepared pan. Press it out with your hands to fill the cake pan.

Proof the dough as described on page 26.

BAKE Just before baking, egg wash according to instructions on page 23. Add pearl sugar to the top after egg washing. Bake in the center of the oven at 350 degrees F for 22 to 25 minutes or until the center is 200 degrees F. Let sit in the pan for 5 minutes before turning it out onto a wire cooling rack. Let cool completely.

TO ASSEMBLE THE TROPÉZIENNE First whip the raspberry ganache. Place all of it in the bowl of a stand mixer fitted with the whisk attachment and whip on medium-high speed until it holds stiff peaks. Put the ganache into a piping bag fitted with a plain tip and set aside.

Now get the black sesame mousseline out and stir well with a spatula to loosen it up a little. Put it in another piping bag fitted with a plain tip and set aside.

With a serrated knife, slice the brioche cake in half horizontally, being careful to keep the knife perfectly parallel to the counter so the

continued

bottom is a nice even thickness. Set the top aside. Brush the bottom round with the raspberry syrup (see photo 1). Along the outer rim of the round, pipe dollops of the fillings, alternating between black sesame mousseline and raspberry whipped ganache (photo 2). In the center, pipe a flat circle of black sesame mousseline that covers the rest of the bottom round, and pipe a flat circle of raspberry whipped ganache on top of that (photos 3 and 4). Press fresh raspberries into the fillings, leaving ½-inch gaps between berries (photo 5).

Place the top half of the brioche on the fillings and raspberries and dust generously with powdered sugar (photo 6). Slice and serve immediately.

NOTE This recipe only requires a half batch of the pillar brioche, but that amount will be difficult to mix properly in the mixer. I suggest you make one full recipe of the pillar brioche, divide it in half after its fridge rest, and roll the excess into dinner rolls. You can proof and bake them like you would the maritozzi buns on page 67, and then brush them with melted butter right out of the oven.

**Makes enough to fill
1 Tropézienne**

125 grams black
  sesame seeds
100 grams sugar,
  divided
Neutral oil, as needed
163 grams milk
28 grams heavy
  cream
90 grams butter
18 grams cornstarch
38 grams egg yolks
  (from 2 to 3 eggs)

Black Sesame Mousseline

This recipe starts with making a black sesame praline, which is then used as a component of a mousseline. Mousseline is basically a custard fortified with praline and butter. You'll make more praline than is required for the mousseline; use leftovers on buttered toast, oatmeal, ice cream, etc. It's amazing!

Preheat the oven to 350 degrees F. Toast the black sesame seeds on a baking sheet for 10 minutes. Let them cool on the baking sheet.

While they cool, make a caramel by putting 75 grams of sugar in a heavy-bottomed pot (preferably copper if you have it) over high heat. Let the sugar cook without stirring until you see the edges liquefy. Begin gently stirring the sugar until it starts to liquify. Continue stirring constantly but gently until you have a dark caramel. Pour this caramel over the sesame seeds immediately and let cool for at least 30 minutes.

When the caramel has hardened, break it apart and toss all the seeds and caramel shards into a food processor. Let the food processor run continuously to grind the seeds and caramel into a paste. If it looks dry and powdery, add 1 teaspoon of neutral oil at a time until it begins to break down into a paste. The sesame praline should look like black tahini when you're done.

continued

Place the milk and cream into a medium pot over medium heat. Put the butter and 100 grams of the sesame praline in a large bowl (set the remainder aside for another use). In a medium bowl, add 25 grams of sugar, the cornstarch, and yolks, and whisk to combine.

Bring the milk and cream to a boil, then temper into the yolk mixture by adding a little of the hot liquid to it, whisking briskly to combine, adding a little more liquid, whisking, and so on until you've added about two-thirds of the hot liquid to the yolks. Turn the heat down to medium, and dump the hot milk/yolk mixture back into the pot, being sure to scrape all of the mixture from the bowl into the pot. Now whisk constantly, being sure to scrape the bottom and sides of the pot as you do so, until the custard thickens. Cook for an additional 30 seconds after it thickens to cook out any raw cornstarch taste.

Pour this custard over the butter and praline, and whisk to combine. It will look a little broken and greasy, which is why you'll now mix it with the immersion blender until it is all emulsified together and looks homogenous. Pour into a bowl or storage container, cover with plastic wrap, and refrigerate overnight or up to 3 days ahead of time.

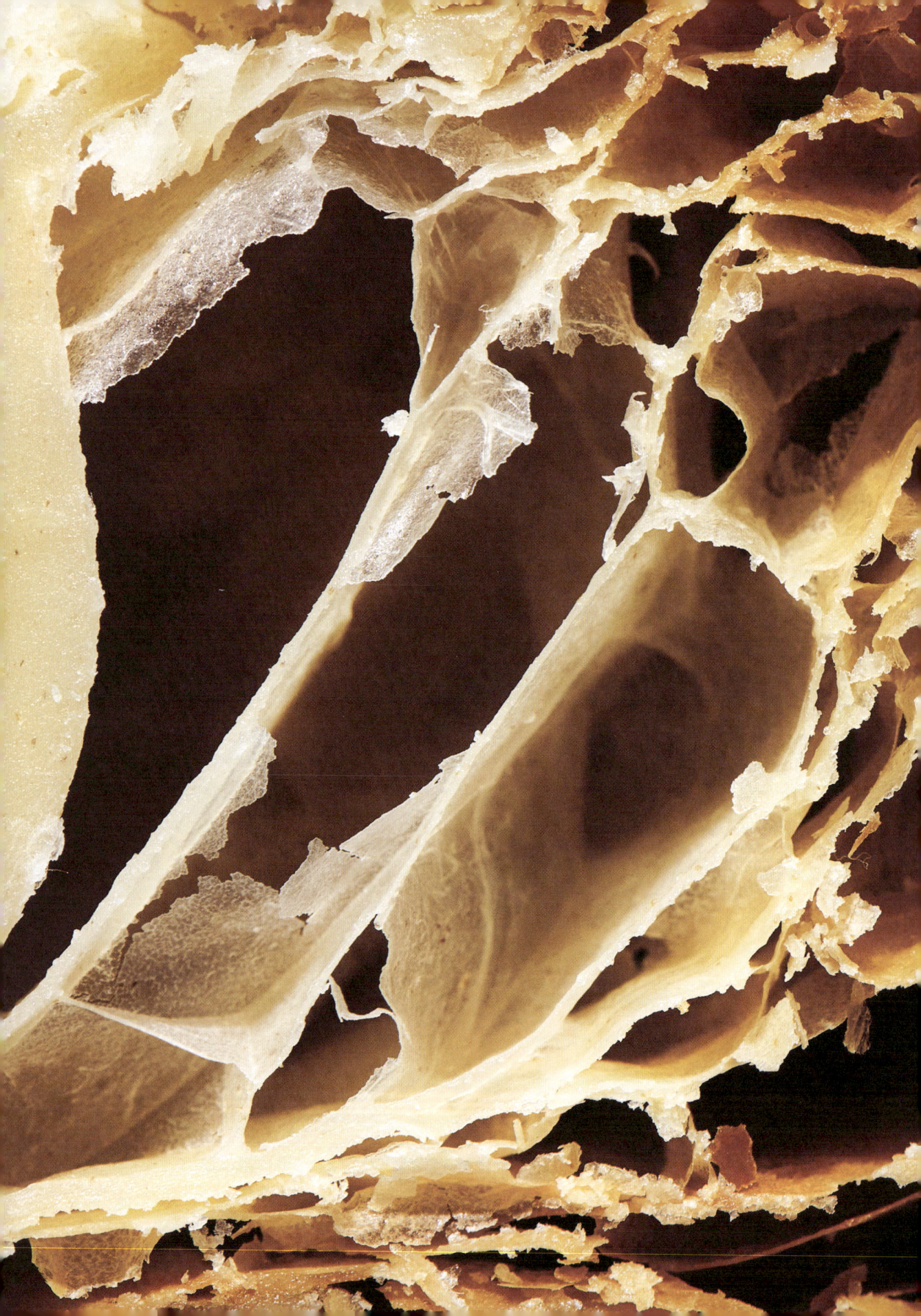

PUFF PASTRY

**P**uff is the most dramatic of the three pillars of pastry. Its rise in the oven is due entirely to steam, as the dough itself is unyeasted. Because of this, its behavior can become erratic without painstaking precision. Let's discuss.

In addition to the dough being unyeasted, it is also extremely stiff, with very low hydration, and very lean, with a super small amount of fat in it. This is going to ensure that when we laminate fat into it, the layers will remain very distinct, despite how thin the layers of dough and butter become. It is important to develop a fair amount of gluten during the mixing process since we will be rolling it out quite thin and stretching it a lot. If gluten is not sufficiently developed, the dough can start to tear when you go to roll it out. And even though this dough doesn't have yeast and therefore requires no extended fermentation, I still rest the dough in the fridge overnight. The dough will become claylike, hard but pliable, and that is the texture you'll need to laminate correctly.

Butter

Now on to the good stuff: the butter! There are multiple ways you can perform the folds on puff pastry to achieve different textures. The fewer folds you do, the thicker and crispier the layers will turn out. You can even make something called inverted puff, where the butter is on the outside and the dough is on the inside! We won't be doing that, though. I prefer four folds for maximum tenderness, which will serve these recipes well. Once you are comfortable with this technique, it might be a fun project to try out different folding patterns to see the difference.

Laminating

When laminating puff, it is so important to make sure the butter is the same thickness throughout and there are equal thicknesses of dough surrounding the butter. The reason it is so important to keep all the layers even is because when the puff goes in the oven, all the layers of butter will begin to melt, and the steam created from that is what pushes the pastry up. If the layers are created unevenly, the rise will also be uneven. This is why, when you make a rough puff, the rise is not very dramatic, and it looks more rustic.

Rolling It Out

Another very important aspect of puff pastry is the thickness, or I should say *thinness,* of the dough when you roll it out. Once lamination is done, do not skimp on rolling the resulting dough out as thin as the recipe requires. This can be challenging at home without a dough sheeter, but it is necessary! If you try to bake puff pastry when it's too thick, it will burst forth in the oven and probably topple over itself, unable to sustain the rapid steam evaporation from thicker layers of butter, and will remain raw in the middle while burning on the outside. If you are struggling to get the dough rolled out thin enough, and it seems like it's just not getting any thinner despite your best efforts, put it on a baking sheet and let it rest in the fridge for 15 minutes. This short rest will relax the dough, and it should behave better once it's had a little nap.

The last thing to note is that because this dough is folded and rolled out so many times, and is already a stiff dough to begin with, it is filled with a lot of tension. If you were to roll it out and then immediately cut it up, the pieces would shrink back, and you'd be left with ovals instead of circles or trapezoids instead of rectangles. To avoid this, you'll need to let the rolled-out dough rest for at least 1 hour before cutting it. If your kitchen is quite cool, you can do this on a floured countertop with plastic wrap over the dough to keep it from drying out. If your kitchen is more than 72 degrees F, place the dough on a baking sheet, cover with plastic wrap, and keep it in the fridge for its rest.

My best advice for puff pastry is "Don't fight your dough." Treat it like a temperamental lover: If things get too tense or you're fighting a lot and getting frustrated, walk away and let the tension dissipate before returning to resolve the issue. The end result will be well worth the effort.

Makes 1 block of puff pastry

For the dough
225 grams cold
  water, plus more for
  adhering
510 grams all-
  purpose flour, plus
  more for dusting
70 grams butter, cold
½ teaspoon freshly
  squeezed lemon
  juice
11 grams salt

For the butter block
500 grams
  high-quality, low-
  moisture, unsalted
  European-style
  butter

PILLAR PUFF PASTRY

I based this recipe off one I learned professionally under James Miller. I will never forget the first time I tasted a puff pastry galette he made; it was simply life-changing. Exquisite in its simplicity, it was just a square of puff topped with lightly macerated rhubarb, then baked and glazed with apricot jam after it came out of the oven. The tenderness of the pastry was what really stuck out to me as it flaked into about seven billion pieces when I took a bite. This recipe is quite similar. I use lemon juice in the dough to keep it from oxidizing in the fridge overnight, and the acidity also lends a small amount of elasticity to the dough. If you don't have fresh lemon juice on hand, you can replace it with white vinegar to get the same results. It's such a small amount that you can't taste it in the final product, but the chemical reaction it provides will be noticeable.

Timeline

DAY ONE mixing puff (20 minutes), resting puff (overnight), making butter block (15 minutes)

DAY TWO laminating puff (2 hours), resting puff (at least 1 hour)

MIX AND SHAPE THE DOUGH Place the water, flour, butter, lemon juice, and salt into the bowl of a stand mixer fitted with the hook attachment.

Mix on low speed for 20 minutes or until the dough is smooth and somewhat elastic. This is a very stiff dough, so you will not be able to do a windowpane test.

Roll into a ball shape, wrap tightly with plastic so no air is touching the dough, and refrigerate overnight.

continued

MAKE THE BUTTER BLOCK AND ROLL OUT THE DOUGH Make the butter block as described on page 16.

Take the butter block out of the refrigerator and let it come to just below room temperature. It should be flexible but still cold. Your main goal here is to get it to the same texture as the dough. You should be able to bend the butter block without it cracking or breaking, but your fingers should not sink into the butter at all.

Take the dough out of the refrigerator and unwrap it, placing it on a lightly floured surface. Lightly dust the dough ball with flour and press very firmly with your rolling pin to create a cross (photo 1).

Starting from the center of the cross, roll each lobe outward to create an 11-by-11-inch square, making sure the dough is of even thickness throughout (photos 2 and 3).

Turn it so it looks like a diamond, then place the butter block in the center (photo 4).

LOCK IN THE BUTTER Take the corners of the dough at the 9:00 and 3:00 positions, and stretch them over the butter block to meet in the middle (photo 5, page 88).

Press firmly to adhere the dough to itself, being careful not to make an indent in the butter. If you're having trouble getting the dough to stick to itself, lightly dab one of the flaps with cold water to help it adhere. Repeat this process with the dough flaps at the 12:00 and 6:00 positions (photo 6).

If there's any butter showing after all the corners are met in the middle, gently stretch the dough edges toward each other to create seams (photo 7).

The butter should be completely enveloped in the dough (photo 8). During this step, try to eliminate all air pockets that could form by hugging the dough very close to the butter. If you notice small air bubbles when you're rolling the dough out, simply pop them with the tip of a paring knife and squish the dough back up close to the butter.

DO THE FIRST FOLD Once the butter is locked in, roll the dough out to create a 9½-by-17-inch rectangle that's about ⅓-inch thick. You should only roll in one direction to lengthen; do not widen. Please note that your dimensions may not completely match up with mine when rolling the dough out, but you should focus on achieving the thickness I'm describing, as that's what is most important.

Trim the short ends to create a nice rectangle shape.

Perform a letter fold as described on page 20.

continued

PASTRY TEMPLE

Cover this dough block with plastic wrap and, with a permanent marker, make a hash mark on the plastic to show you've done the first fold. Let the dough rest in the refrigerator for 30 minutes.

ROLL OUT THE DOUGH Take your dough out of the refrigerator and position it so the spine is to your left. Gently but firmly roll it out, moving the rolling pin away from you and toward you to lengthen the dough until it is about 5½ by 29 inches and ⅓-inch thick.

If your dough sticks to the surface at all, lightly dust with flour. You'll want to avoid adding so much flour that the dough slides around, but you definitely don't want it to stick and tear as you roll it out.

PERFORM THE BOOK FOLDS Perform a book fold as described on page 19.

Rotate the dough so its spine is to your left again. Roll it out as before, lengthening it to about 9 by 18 inches and ⅓-inch thick.

Perform another book fold, then wrap in plastic. Make two more hash marks on it to show you've done the second and third folds, then let rest in the refrigerator for 30 minutes.

DO THE LAST FOLD Take the dough out again, and, you guessed it, turn it so the spine is to your left. Roll it out (again!) to about 6 by 24 inches and ⅓-inch thick.

Do a letter fold as described on page 20, then refrigerate, wrapped in plastic, for at least 1 hour.

At this point, it's done. You can tightly double-wrap it in plastic and keep it in the fridge for up to 2 days. Or, as I prefer to do, after its fridge rest you can roll it out to the thickness needed for the recipes you want to make with it, portion it out, and freeze each one for up to 2 months. Just make sure they are tightly double-wrapped and labeled so you don't forget what you rolled them out for. When you're ready to bake the dough, let it thaw in the refrigerator overnight; never let it thaw at room temperature.

1 recipe Pillar Puff
  Pastry (page 85)
Flour, for dusting

For the filling
300 grams cream
  cheese, at room
  temperature
30 grams furikake
  seasoning (see Note
  on page 92)
3 scallions, thinly
  sliced on a bias
120 grams smoked
  salmon

For the egg wash
1 egg yolk
2 tablespoons heavy
  cream or milk

Furikake Smoked Salmon Puffs

Ever since I was a small child, I have been obsessed with small hors d'oeuvres. I'm not sure why, but the thought of two-bite little treats being passed around on trays at a party is just so delightful to me. A classic example of one of these is a salmon puff, a pastry filled with cooked salmon and cream cheese and maybe spinach as well: a relic of the 1980s! While I love the concept of this, I had to put a modern twist on it and bring some true Pacific Northwest flavor to it. I swapped the cooked salmon for smoked salmon, which has a much stronger flavor packed with umami. The cream cheese includes furikake, a nod to the Asian American Pacific Islander influence on Seattle's food scene. These would be perfect to serve at your next soiree.

Special equipment needed

3-inch cookie cutter

Timeline

Shaping pastries (20 minutes), making filling (30 minutes), baking pastries (30 minutes)

PREPARE THE PUFF PASTRY After the dough's final fridge rest, roll the dough out to ¼-inch thickness. Using 3-inch cookie cutters, cut out twenty-four rounds of dough. Place them on a lightly floured baking sheet, cover in plastic wrap, and put in the fridge to stay cold while you make the filling. Save any unused dough for another purpose or for a scrap packet recipe.

MAKE THE FILLING In a medium bowl, mix the cream cheese, furikake, and scallions together until smooth and evenly distributed. Gently fold in the smoked salmon, keeping the fish in small chunks rather than completely breaking it down into a paste.

continued

Place half of the circles on a parchment-lined baking sheet. Poke them all over with a fork; this is called docking. Docking will create extra steam vents in the pastry and help prevent the bottoms from puffing up too much and toppling the entire pastry over in the oven. Spoon about 2 tablespoons of the filling into the center of each circle, leaving a small border of plain dough all around the circumference.

Brush each border very lightly with egg wash (see instructions on page 23) or cold water, then press the rest of the undocked circles down over the tops. Leaving the pastry on the baking sheet, secure the tops to the bottoms along that border with your (now dry) fingers or the tines of a fork, pressing very firmly to adhere. Be careful not to let the filling ooze out the sides, and try to eliminate all air pockets from the equation. Once they're all paired up and assembled, pop them back in the fridge to stay cold.

Preheat the oven to 375 degrees F. Use the tip of a sharp paring knife to poke a hole in the top of each pastry. This will vent the steam coming out of the pastry and the filling and help it rise a little more evenly. Don't go overboard with this step though. Just a small hole is sufficient; too big a hole will split the pastry open in the oven.

Just before baking, egg wash according to instructions on page 23. Bake for 30 minutes or until the pastry is a deep golden brown. Let cool for at least 15 minutes before serving.

NOTE Furikake is a mixture of sesame seeds, bonito flakes, and dried seaweed, and it can be found in Asian grocery stores or online. It comes in a variety of flavors, so choose one that sounds appealing to you.

Makes 1 large tart,
6 to 8 servings
as an appetizer

1 recipe Pillar Puff
  Pastry (page 85)
Flour, for dusting
Olive oil, for drizzling
Shaved parmesan, for
  garnishing

For the filling
120 grams bacon
220 grams leeks
  (about 2 medium
  leeks)
Salt and freshly
  ground black
  pepper

For the pickled leeks
1 teaspoon salt
White wine vinegar,
  for pickling

For the crème fraîche
75 grams crème
  fraîche
1 clove garlic, grated
¼ teaspoon salt
⅛ teaspoon freshly
  ground black
  pepper

For egg wash
1 egg yolk
2 tablespoons heavy
  cream or milk

Bacon Leek Tart

This pastry makes a great appetizer for a dinner party. I have always enjoyed the combination of melted leeks and smoky bacon, and the pickled leeks add a little necessary punch of acidity and crunch to an otherwise rich starter. This recipe will make more pickled leeks than you'll need for the tart; they're a great addition to salads, grain bowls, and roasted meats, and they will keep in the fridge for up to two weeks.

Timeline

DAY ONE mixing puff (25 minutes)

DAY TWO laminating puff (2 hours), making filling (30 to 45 minutes), shaping pastry (20 minutes), baking pastry (30 minutes)

Prepare the puff pastry. After the dough's final fridge rest, roll it out to ¼-inch thickness, and cut a 6-by-12-inch rectangle from it. Place it on a lightly floured baking sheet, cover in plastic wrap, and put in the fridge to stay cold while you make the filling. Save the remaining dough for another purpose.

MAKE THE FILLING Dice the bacon into ½-inch pieces and put in a skillet over medium heat. Cook, stirring occasionally, until the fat has rendered and the bacon is slightly crispy but not hardened. Transfer to a paper towel-lined plate. Drain off all but 2 tablespoons of the bacon fat.

Slice the leeks lengthwise to rinse the dirt out, then slice crosswise into thin strips. You'll only want to use the white and light green parts of the leeks; save the darker green parts for pickling.

Heat the reserved bacon fat over medium high and add the leeks. Cook, stirring often, until water starts to come out of the leeks. Keep cooking, making sure the leeks don't stick to the pan, until the water has evaporated and the pan is dry. Add a few pinches of salt to draw out more moisture, and continue to cook until the second round of water has been extracted and evaporated. Transfer to a bowl and mix in the bacon. Season to taste with salt and pepper and let cool completely.

MAKE THE PICKLED LEEKS Very thinly slice the reserved dark green part of the leeks. Place in a small bowl, massage with the salt until tender, and then cover with the vinegar. Set aside until ready to use or for up to 24 hours in the fridge.

MAKE THE CRÈME FRAÎCHE In a small bowl, mix the crème fraîche, garlic, salt, and pepper. Taste and adjust seasoning to your liking. Refrigerate until needed.

Preheat the oven to 375 degrees F. Line a baking sheet with parchment paper and place the puff pastry on it.

Following the scoring instructions on page 23, score the pastry down both of the long sides, making one line on each side, 1 inch in from the border. In the middle 4-inch section, take a fork and poke several holes in the pastry to dock it. This will allow the border of the tart to rise evenly while the middle stays flat to hold the filling.

Spread the crème fraîche mixture evenly over the middle section of the tart. Then place the bacon-leek filling over the top of the crème fraîche, and drizzle lightly with olive oil. Brush the borders with egg wash (see instructions on page 23). You can decoratively score the borders or leave them plain.

Bake for 30 minutes or until the pastry is a deep golden brown and the filling has taken on some color. Let cool for 10 minutes, then garnish with the parmesan and pickled leeks. Slice crosswise to serve.

1 recipe Pillar Puff
  Pastry (page 85)
Flour, for dusting

For the filling
700 grams ground
  pork
50 grams minced
  shallot (about
  1 medium shallot)
20 grams minced
  garlic (about
  5 small cloves)
20 grams palm sugar
  or brown sugar
20 grams fish sauce
1 stalk lemongrass,
  tough outer leaves
  discarded and
  tender stalk minced
¼ cup chopped
  cilantro
1 medium jalapeño,
  finely chopped
20 grams salt

For the egg wash
1 egg yolk
2 tablespoons heavy
  cream or milk

Banh Mi Sausage Roll

I have always been somewhat obsessed with Australia, and I was lucky enough to visit Melbourne and Sydney recently. While there, I ate at a restaurant that served banh mi pâté en croûte, which is pressed, flavored pâté inside a pastry crust. It was absolutely incredible. So this recipe is an homage to that dish, with an even more Australian twist added to it in the form of their beloved sausage roll. This is great served with pickled carrots and radishes alongside.

Timeline

DAY ONE making filling (30 minutes plus at least one hour to chill)

DAY TWO shaping pastry (20 minutes), baking pastry (1 hour)

Prepare the puff pastry. After the dough's final fridge rest, roll it out to ¼-inch thickness and cut a 14-by-12-inch rectangle from it. Place it on a lightly floured baking sheet, cover in plastic wrap, and put in the fridge to stay cold while you make the filling. Save the remaining dough for another purpose.

MAKE THE FILLING In a medium bowl, add the pork, shallot, garlic, sugar, fish sauce, lemongrass, cilantro, jalapeño, and salt. Mix gently with your hands until all the ingredients are evenly distributed. Try not to overwork the meat or it will become tough and spongy.

Roll out a length of plastic wrap and turn the sausage mixture onto it. Firmly form the sausage into a 12-inch-long cylinder. Make it as even as possible. Roll very tightly with the plastic wrap several times to create a log shape. Refrigerate for at least 1 hour to firm up, up to overnight.

The tighter you're able to wrap the sausage, the better this pastry will turn out. Don't be afraid to wrap it multiple times to create a very tight seal and get as much air out as you possibly can.
Preheat the oven to 400 degrees F.

continued

Place the puff pastry sheet on a lightly floured surface with the longer side toward you. Lightly brush the two-thirds closest to you with egg wash (see instructions on page 23), and put the unwrapped sausage roll on the border closest to you. You should have a 1-inch border on either side of the roll. Very firmly roll the pastry around the sausage, leaving no air gaps between the meat and the dough. Once the sausage is fully enclosed in the pastry, you should be left with a short overhang; that's good! Carefully fold the two open ends like you would wrap a present, first folding in the two sides, then bringing up the bottom, then the top down over the rest. Press firmly on the seals of the dough to close it up.

Egg wash the entire pastry according to the instructions on page 23 and put it back in the fridge for 10 minutes to get cold again. Lightly score the round part of the cylinder by running the tip of a sharp paring knife over it at 2-inch increments, kind of so it looks like a barber pole. Scoring this dough will help it expand in the oven without tearing. Be careful not to cut all the way through the dough, just a few layers of it; no sausage should be showing through the cuts. Score the overhang decoratively as well. Bake for 1 hour or until the pastry is a golden-brown color and the internal temperature of the pork is at least 160 degrees F.

Carefully transfer the pastry to a cooling rack and let cool for 10 to 15 minutes. Cut off the ends, slice the log into 1-inch-wide rounds, and serve.

1 recipe Pillar Puff
  Pastry (page 85)
Flour, for dusting
100 grams butter,
  softened
100 grams brown
  sugar
100 grams feta
  cheese, crumbled
Fresh parsley,
  for garnish

For the filling
1200 grams sweet
  potatoes
10 oz Harissa paste
Salt

Harissa-Sweet Potato Rosette Tart
with Feta

When I was in my twenties, I spent six years as a vegetarian. This coincided with my blossoming interest in making food, and I remember falling in love with savory tarts. This dish has a subtle, sweet earthiness from sweet potatoes that pairs well with the punchy spice from harissa paste. Buttery puff pastry and briny feta bring it all together to make a satisfying vegetarian dish. Taking the time to layer the slices of sweet potato in a rosette pattern makes this pastry beautiful enough to grace a Thanksgiving dinner tablescape.

Special equipment

Mandoline, ovenproof 9-inch skillet such as cast iron or stainless steel

Timeline

Making filling (30 to 45 minutes), shaping pastry (30 minutes), baking pastry (1 hour)

Prepare the puff pastry. After the dough's final fridge rest, roll it to ¼-inch thickness and cut a 10-inch circle out of it. Place it on a lightly floured baking sheet, cover in plastic wrap, and put in the fridge to stay cold while you make the filling. Save the remaining dough for another purpose.

MAKE THE FILLING Peel the sweet potatoes and carefully slice them lengthwise at ⅛ inch thick on a mandoline, or use a very sharp knife. You'll end up with long, flexible ribbons of sweet potato. Stack the ribbons and cut them in half lengthwise. This will give them a straight edge to work with. Lay them all out on a work surface and spread harissa paste on both sides of each piece; season with salt.

Smear the softened butter in a 9-inch ovenproof skillet. Get the bottom and sides coated well. Sprinkle the brown sugar evenly over the bottom of the pan.

continued on page 102

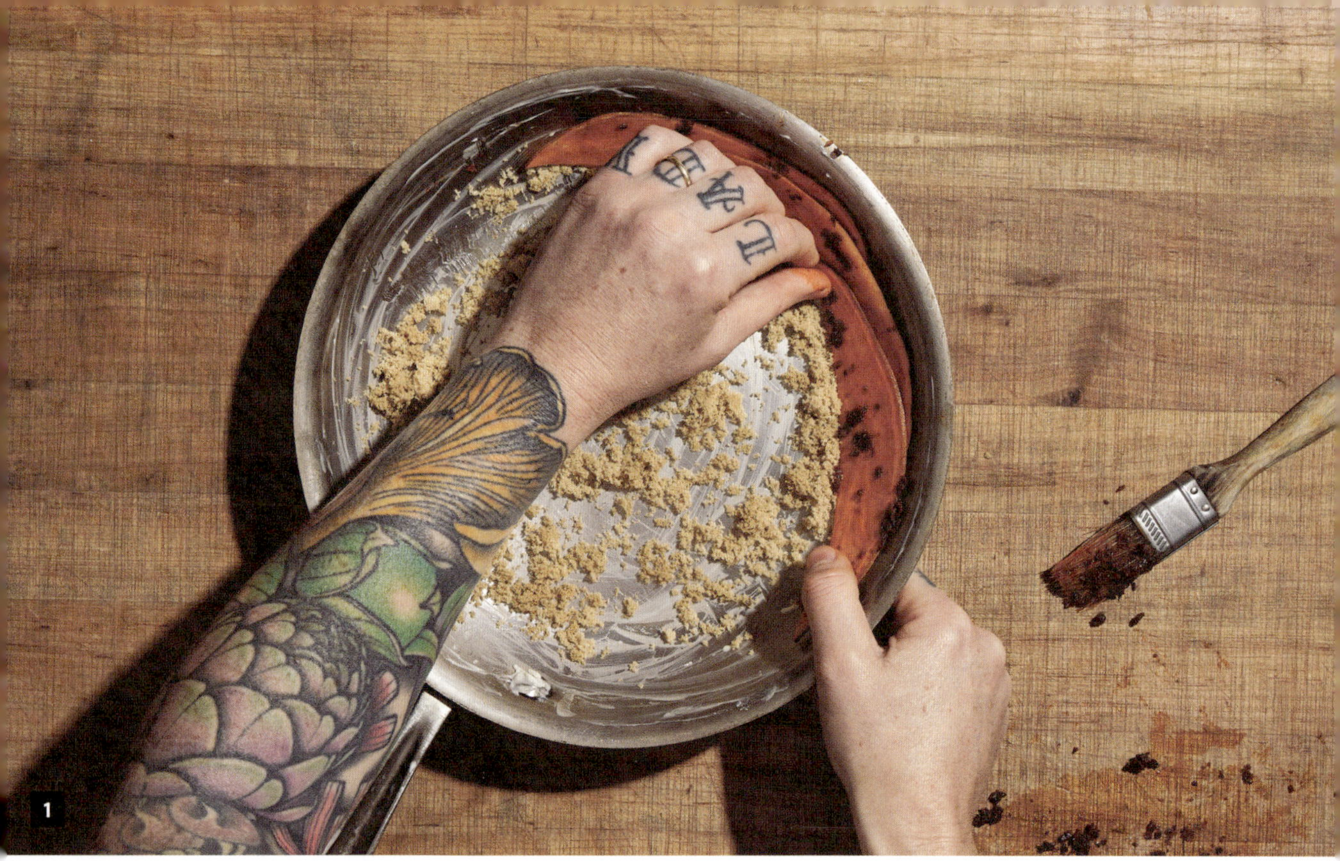
1

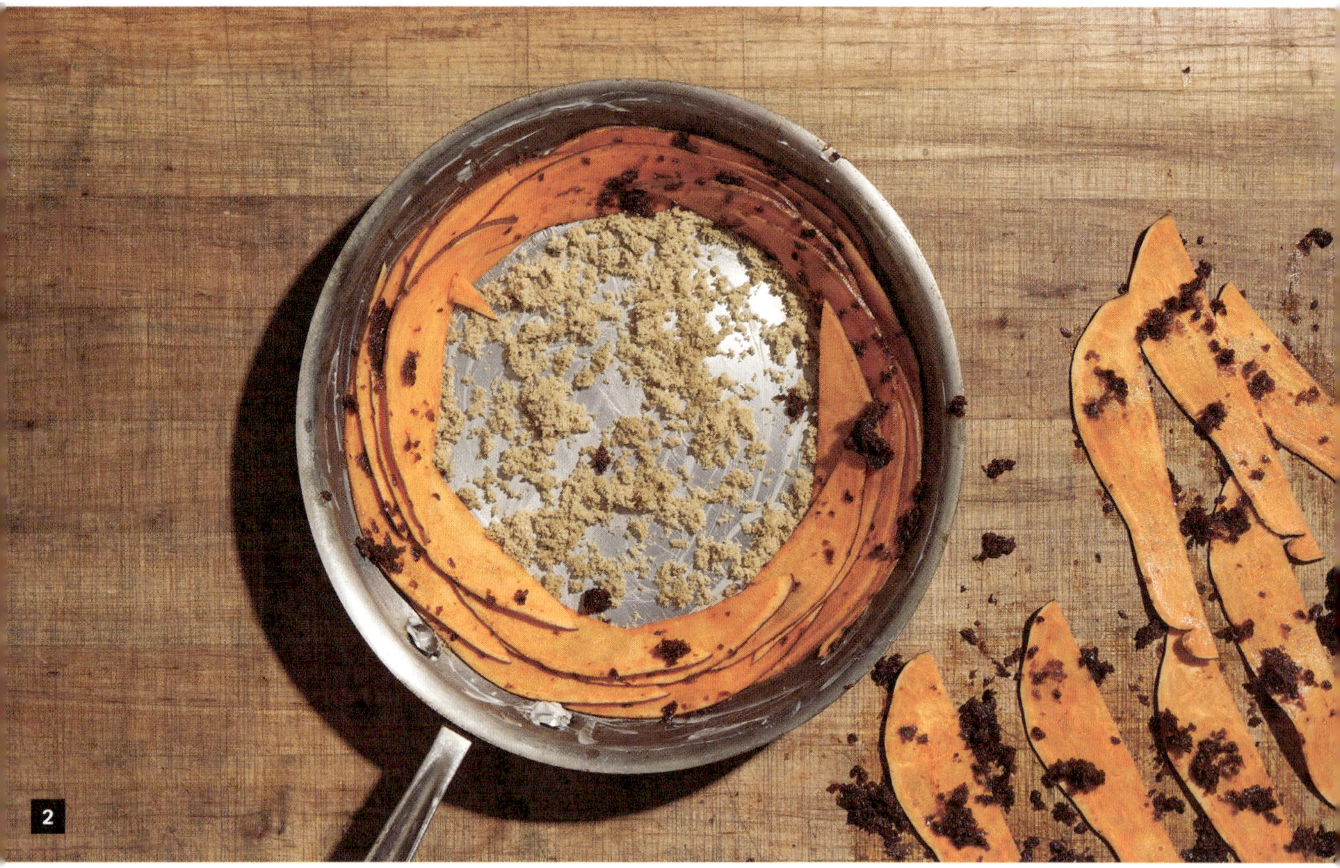
2

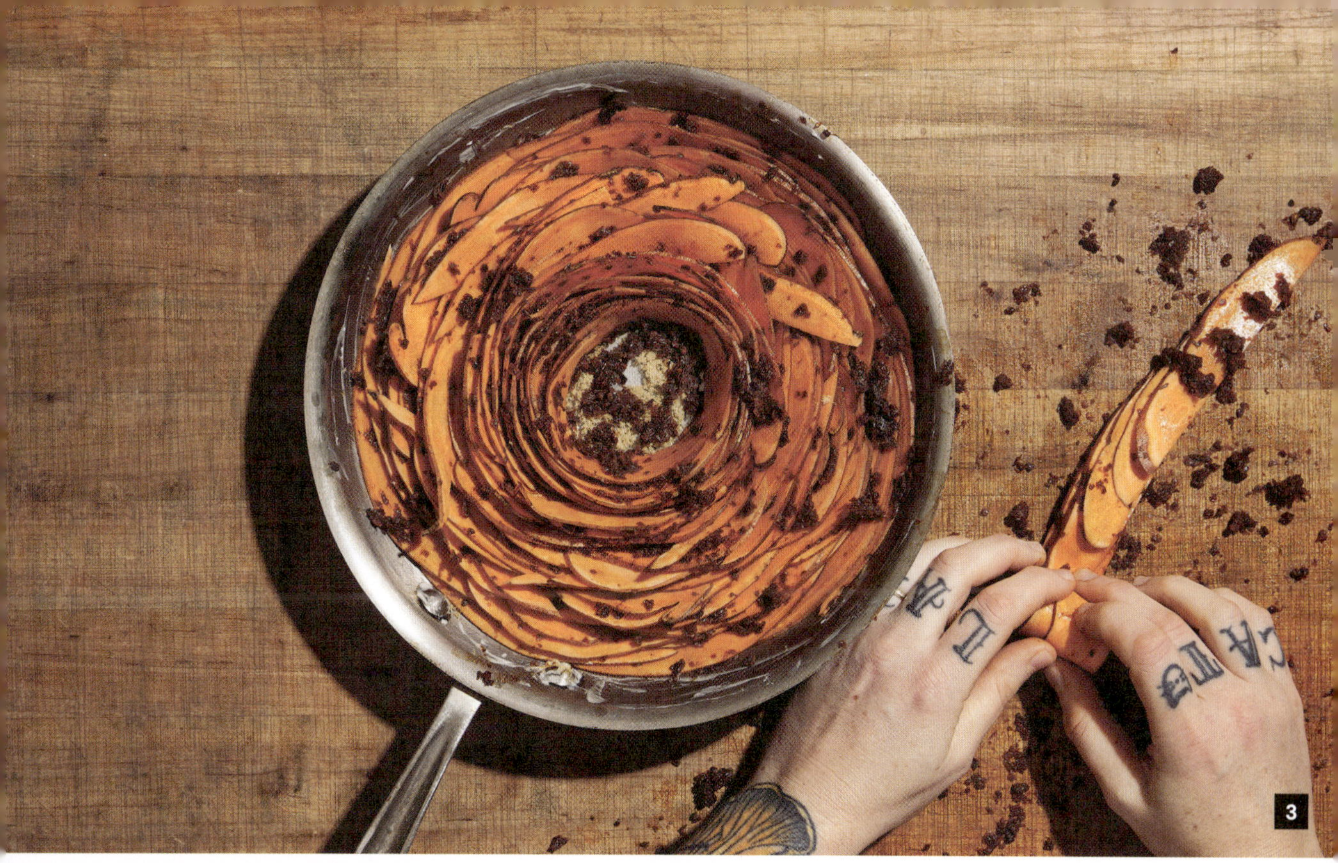
3

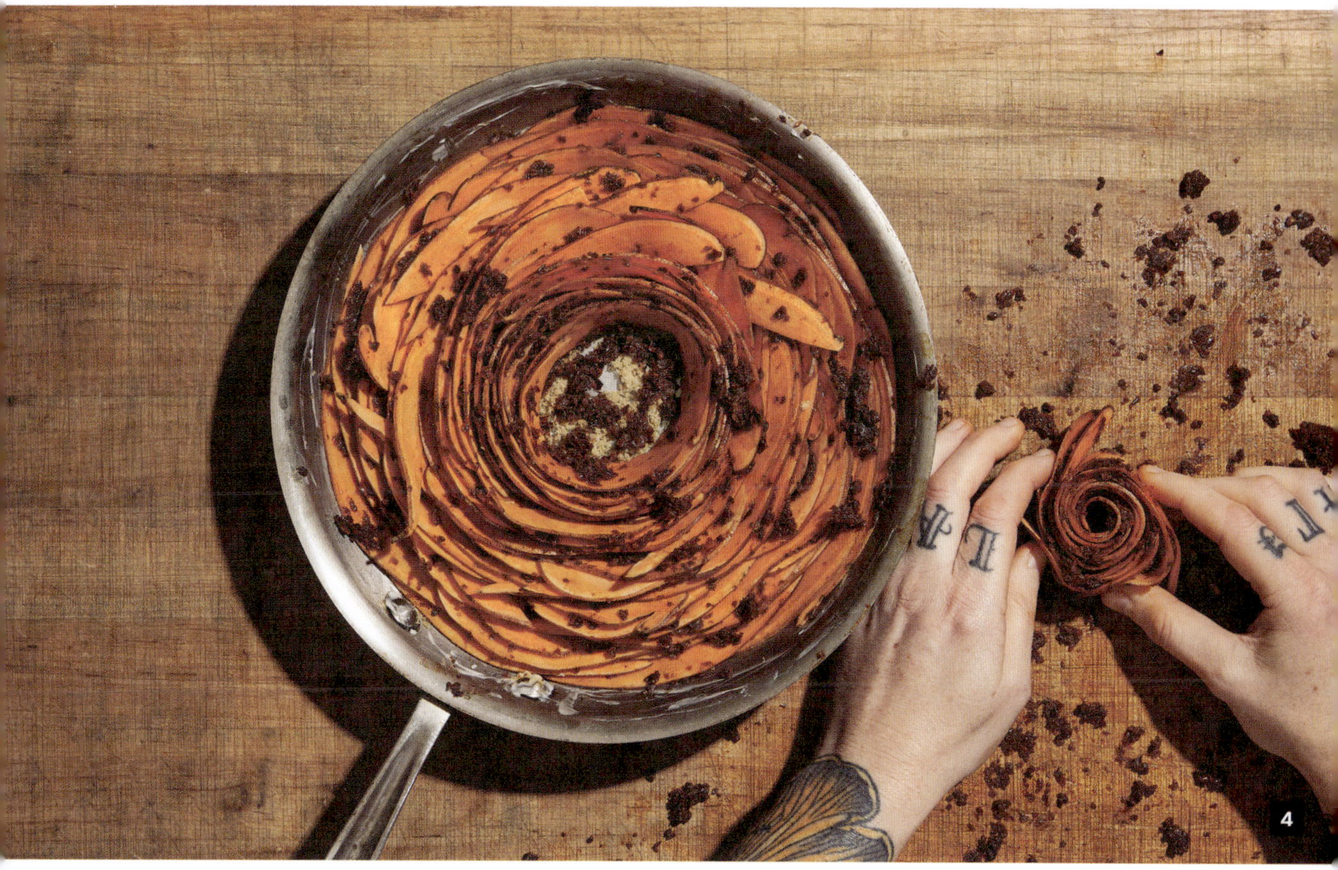
4

Preheat the oven to 350 degrees F.

In the prepared skillet, begin arranging a few strips of the sweet potato around the outside edge, slightly overlapping the strips (photo 1). Keep working inward, creating a kind of rose shape with the potatoes, getting them as tightly packed in as you can (photo 2). When you are approaching the center of the pan, lay some potato petals out on the counter and overlap them. Then roll them up (photo 3) into a rose shape and place that in the open center of the skillet (photo 4).

Take the pastry round out of the fridge and drape it over the skillet. You should have a slight overhang; gently fold the overhang into the skillet so it cradles the filling. Poke four or five holes in the pastry to help it vent steam in the oven. Bake for 1 hour or until the crust is a deep golden brown.

Let cool for 10 minutes. Place a plate upside down over the top of the skillet and carefully invert the tart onto the plate. Garnish with crumbles of feta and parsley leaves. Serve at room temperature.

Buckwheat Palmiers

For the dough
225 grams cold water
400 grams all-
  purpose flour, plus
  more for dusting
110 grams buckwheat
  flour
70 grams cold
  European-style
  butter
½ teaspoon freshly
  squeezed lemon
  juice
11 grams salt

For the butter block
500 grams
  European-style
  butter
250 grams sugar,
  plus more for
  coating

When starting my croissant pop-up business, I had an intense focus on using nontraditional grains in my pastries. I did this partly as a way to distinguish myself but also because I am a firm believer in diversity in all aspects of life. Biodiversity is critically important to the health of our soil, food system, and own gut microbiome. The dearth of grain diversity in baking I think is partly due to lack of exposure to such grains. Once people try them, they fall in love, but the first step is to make something delicious with them so the demand for that grain grows. Buckwheat is a great place to start since it has such a strong, earthy flavor. Buckwheat pairs well with chocolate and tart fruits, such as lemon. Think of its flavor profile like a beet, and anything that would go well with beets will likely fit right in with buckwheat. These palmiers have been on the menu at Temple Pastries since our opening, and they remain one of my favorite afternoon treats. The addition of buckwheat flour gives the dough a beautiful speckled color and brings a delightful earthiness to it that I honestly can't get enough of.

Timeline

Shaping pastries (20 minutes), baking pastries (30 minutes)

MAKE THE DOUGH Mix the cold water, both flours, butter, lemon juice, and salt exactly as described in Pillar Puff Pastry (page 85).

Make the butter block as described on page 16. Laminate the dough as described on page 82.

Once the dough is laminated, roll it into a 16-by-12-inch rectangle that is a little less than ¼ inch thick. Carefully trim a small amount off the top and bottom borders. Now visually divide the dough into four equal strips going lengthwise. Cover the middle two quarters with sugar. Be generous here; you don't want any dough showing through the sugar. With the 12-inch side closest to you, fold the bottom quarter

continued

up over half of the sugared part to land in the middle. Repeat with the top quarter. Now cover the top half with sugar, again being generous so that no dough shows through the sugar. Fold the bottom half up over the top half. You should be left with a log of dough that is about 4 inches wide. Refrigerate this log of dough for 15 minutes if the dough has gotten warm.

Place the log back onto a counter with the spine toward you. Trim off one of the edges. Measure ¾-inch increments from that first cut, and slice at each mark. Dip both of the cut edges into a bowl of sugar to coat and put on a parchment-lined baking sheet in the fridge.

When you're ready to bake, preheat the oven to 350 degrees F. You can fit about four of these palmiers on a standard baking sheet; spread them out accordingly as they'll expand quite a bit in the oven.

Bake for 30 minutes, flipping them over halfway through so they caramelize evenly. Let cool completely before enjoying. Any unbaked pastries can be kept wrapped airtight in the freezer for up to 1 month. You can bake them straight from the freezer and be snacking on them with an espresso in half an hour—the perfect little afternoon treat!

Makes 8 pastries

1 recipe Pillar Puff
    Pastry (page 85)
Flour, for dusting

For the filling
500 grams plums
    (7 to 9 plums)
200 grams sugar
8 green cardamom
    pods, crushed

For the egg wash
1 egg yolk
2 tablespoons heavy
    cream or milk

Plum-Cardamom Chausson

I have always been in love with fruit. As a kid, it was unfortunately limited to canned pears and peaches, although I still have a nostalgic soft spot for those! In Florida, I was very keen on mangoes and lychee brought to me from friends in Miami. But Seattle has really got some of the best fruits around. Rhubarb in people's gardens! Berry brambles on the sidewalks! Plum trees everywhere! I don't think I'd ever had a plum until I moved to Seattle, and now you cannot keep me away from them. Late summer is when you can find the best stone fruit, but this recipe will also work with less-than-ideal plums, as roasting them first will concentrate all their flavor. The term *chausson* is almost exclusively used to refer to chaussons aux pommes, a French version of an apple turnover, which literally translates to "apple slippers." The decorated half-moon shape of these pastries is supposedly reminiscent of French slippers, and although I'm not quite sure I see the resemblance, I do love the shape for its ability to hold fruity fillings of all kinds.

Special equipment

Immersion blender

Timeline

DAY ONE Macerating plums (5 minutes plus overnight)

DAY TWO Making filling (45 minutes to 1 hour), shaping pastries (30 minutes), baking pastries (30 minutes)

Prepare the puff pastry. After the dough's final fridge rest, roll it out to ⅛-inch thickness and cut out eight 6-inch rounds from it. Place them on a lightly floured baking sheet, cover in plastic wrap, and put in the fridge to stay cold while you make the filling. Save any remaining dough for another use.

continued

MAKE THE FILLING Dice the plums into 1-inch pieces and toss with the sugar and cardamom pods. Let macerate in a covered container in the refrigerator overnight.

After macerating, preheat the oven to 350 degrees F.

Pick out the cardamom pods from the plums and discard; scrape everything else into an ovenproof skillet and cook over medium heat. Once the mixture is simmering, transfer it to the oven. Cook for 45 minutes to 1 hour, stirring every 15 minutes, until the liquid has reduced to a syrupy consistency and coats the back of a spoon. Immersion blend the fruit to make a jam. You can keep it a little chunky or puree until smooth; that's completely up to your personal taste. Let cool completely.

Preheat the oven to 375 degrees F. Line a baking sheet with parchment paper.

Lightly flour a work surface and gently roll each circle of dough into an oval that's 8 inches long. Only roll in one direction (toward and away from you) to create the oval shape. With a fork, lightly dock half of the oval. Work with one pastry round at a time, keeping the others in the refrigerator to stay cold.

Remove the pastry ovals from the refrigerator and put them on the prepared baking sheet. Put about 2 tablespoons of plum jam on the docked half of each pastry, making sure to leave a border of at least ¾ inch. Use less jam if you need to achieve that border.

Wet your finger and run it along the border of each pastry. Fold the undocked half of each pastry over the jam and press firmly with your fingers to adhere the top to the bottom border, doing your best to eliminate air pockets.

Egg wash according to instructions on page 23 and pop the whole baking sheet in the freezer for 5 minutes.

Once the egg wash sets a bit on the pastry and becomes tacky to the touch, 3 to 5 minutes, take a paring knife and create five vent holes in the top of each pastry. Score decoratively with the knife, then bake for 30 minutes or until golden brown. Let cool for at least 15 minutes before serving.

You can try these other combinations, but note that the baking times for the jam and the amounts of spices needed may vary:

- Pear and star anise
- Nectarine and fresh lavender
- Cherry and vanilla bean

- Blackberry and basil
- Loquat and allspice

Hazelnut Galette de Rois

Makes 1 large galette, 8 to 10 servings

1 recipe Pillar Puff Pastry (page 85)
Flour, for dusting
Porcelain fève or large dried bean (for fun, completely optional)

For the filling

100 grams hazelnuts (about ½ cup)
100 grams powdered sugar
100 grams butter, at room temperature
4 grams cornstarch
4 grams salt
50 grams egg (about 1 egg)

For the egg wash

1 egg yolk
2 tablespoons heavy cream or milk

Part of what I love about pastry is its deep roots in history, particularly related to religious festivals. It's something to be eaten on a special occasion, this cake in particular. Galette de rois, or king cake, is eaten in Europe for Epiphany to celebrate the three wise men visiting baby Jesus. Inside the cake is a small porcelain fève, or figurine, and whoever gets the piece with this in it is supposed to get good luck for the year. But this pastry goes back even further to Roman times and the cult of Saturnalia, where instead of a fève, there was a dried bean inside (*fève* means "bean" in French; this is where the term originated). Whoever received it got to be king for a day, surpassing all social strata. What a day that must have been!

Special equipment

Towel, food processor, perforated silicone baking mat (see Note on page 111) or wire cooling rack and 2-inch-tall ramekins

Timeline

DAY ONE Making filling (45 minutes, plus overnight to chill)

DAY TWO Assembling pastry (10 to 15 minutes, plus one hour to chill), baking pastry (1 hour)

Prepare the puff pastry. After the dough's final fridge rest, roll the dough out to ⅛-inch thickness and cut two 9½-inch rounds out of it. Place them on a lightly floured baking sheet, cover in plastic wrap, and put in the fridge to stay cold while you make the filling. Save the remaining dough for another use.

MAKE THE FILLING Preheat the oven to 350 degrees F. Toast the hazelnuts on a baking sheet for 15 minutes or until deeply golden brown.

Let cool and then rub off the skins with a clean towel. Once the nuts are completely cooled, process them in a food processor with the sugar to create a hazelnut meal. The pieces should be like ground coffee in texture.

In a stand mixer fitted with the paddle attachment, mix the butter, hazelnut meal, cornstarch, and salt together on medium-low speed until smooth; do not incorporate air into the mixture. Add the egg and mix on low speed until incorporated, scraping down the bowl to make sure everything is homogenous. Transfer to a container and refrigerate overnight to firm up.

Place one pastry round on a parchment-lined baking sheet. Spread the hazelnut filling evenly over the pastry round, leaving a 1-inch border all around the edge. Lightly press the fève into the filling anywhere toward the outer edge of the filling. Wet the edge slightly with your finger and some water.

Dock the second pastry round all over with a fork. Gently place the docked round on top of the filling and firmly adhere to the moistened border of the bottom round. You can use a fork to really press them together if you're worried about the filling leaking out. Try to avoid air pockets between the pastry and filling. Transfer the baking sheet to the freezer and let chill for at least 1 hour, up to overnight.

Preheat the oven to 375 degrees F.

Take the galette out of the freezer and invert it so the docked portion is on the bottom. Brush the flat top with egg wash (see instructions on page 23).

Use a paring knife to create a vent hole in the center and four to six others across the top. Score the galette decoratively. If left unchecked, this puff pastry will rise in all sorts of unruly ways in the oven, so we'll need to create a top barrier for it to bump up against to have it bake evenly and come out looking flat and beautiful. If you have a perforated baking mat, place it directly on top of the pastry. It needs to be perforated to let steam escape; a standard silicon mat will trap moisture and you'll end up with a soggy mess. If you don't have one, place two ramekins in opposite corners of the baking sheet and put a wire cooling rack on top of them. Weigh the rack down with more ramekins.

Bake for 50 minutes to 1 hour or until the pastry is a deep golden color. Transfer to a wire rack to cool and serve at room temperature.

NOTE You can purchase perforated silicone mats at BakeDeco.com. They are a small investment but also work well for baking completely flat shortbread cookies and tart shells.

1 recipe Pillar Puff
    Pastry (page 85)
Flour, for dusting

For the filling
600 to 700 grams
    quinces (5 to 6 large
    quinces or pears)
Sugar, for poaching
Freshly squeezed
    juice of 1 large
    lemon

For the caramel
175 grams sugar
80 grams butter, cut
    into small cubes
1 vanilla bean, seeds
    scraped out and
    pod reserved for
    another use

Poached Quince Tarte Tatin

Quince is a fruit I had never heard of prior to moving to Seattle, and it's a strange one to be sure. They are hard and round and a little knobby, and don't try to eat one raw as they are super astringent until cooked. They're a pain to peel and grow for only about six weeks a year, but if handled properly, they are the most luscious, velvety, perfumed fruit you've ever tasted, and it will be well worth the effort. They turn a beautiful deep pink color when poached, and they taste like an apple, a pear, and a rose all had a love child together. If you can't find quince, slightly underripe and very firm Bosc or Anjou pears will work in their place. Whipped crème fraiche or vanilla ice cream make great accoutrements.

Special equipment

9-inch ovenproof skillet, preferably cast iron or stainless steel

Timeline

DAY ONE Poaching quinces (30 minutes to 1 hour)

DAY TWO Making caramel (30 minutes), shaping pastry (15 minutes), baking pastry (1 hour)

Prepare the puff pastry. After the dough's final fridge rest, roll it out to ⅛-inch thickness and cut a 10-inch circle out of it. Place on a lightly floured baking sheet, cover with plastic wrap, and put in the fridge to stay cold while you make the filling. Save any extra dough for another use.

MAKE THE FILLING Peel and quarter the quince. Put them in a wide, shallow pot.

Fill a large container with water and weigh it. Add enough of this water to the pot to cover the quinces by a ½ inch, weigh the container again, and note how much water you used.

Add the same amount of sugar (by weight) to the pot as you did water. Add the lemon juice to the pot.

continued

Bring the pot to a boil over medium heat, then immediately reduce to a very slight simmer, stirring occasionally to make sure the quinces at the bottom of the pot don't cook faster than the ones at the top. Cook very gently, stirring occasionally, until the quinces are easily pierced with the tip of a knife: 30 minutes to 1 hour, depending on how ripe and large the quinces are.

Transfer the quinces to a plate to cool separately from the syrup. Once they're cool enough to handle, cut the core out of the center of each quince. Cool the poaching liquid as well. Place the quince quarters in a container and cover with the cold poaching liquid. Cover and refrigerate until you're ready to use or for up to 1 week.

MAKE THE CARAMEL In a heavy-bottomed saucepan, preferably copper if you have it, heat the sugar over high heat without stirring. Once the edges of the sugar begin to liquefy, you can start to gently stir the sugar. Keep stirring, gently and slowly, until the sugar turns into a dark golden caramel. Lower the heat if this is happening too fast for comfort.

Once the caramel is golden, turn the heat down to medium and add the butter and vanilla bean seeds. It will bubble up some, so use caution. Whisk carefully but briskly to incorporate the butter into the caramel. Once you don't see any more melted butter floating on the caramel, immediately pour it into the skillet you'll be baking the tart in and let cool.

Preheat the oven to 350 degrees F.

Drain the quinces and let them dry out on paper towels, patting them dry all over. Once the caramel has cooled, arrange the quince quarters cut side up in the skillet. Nestle them closely together, overlapping slightly if needed. You want them nice and snug.

Carefully drape the pastry over the skillet and tuck the overhang in so it surrounds the quince. Poke four to five venting holes in the top of the pastry with a paring knife. Bake for 1 hour or until the pastry is a deep golden brown.

Let cool in the skillet for 15 minutes, then place a plate upside down over the top of the pastry and very carefully but quickly invert the pastry onto the plate. I did this over the sink in case any caramel dripped out in the process. Move with speed and confidence to make this easier. Let cool for another 15 minutes and then serve.

NOTE Leftover quince poaching liquid makes a great addition to cocktails. Add it to plain soda water with a squeeze of lemon for a refreshing nonalcoholic drink.

Makes about
12 to 36 twists,
depending on
how much puff
pastry scrap
you have

Puff pastry
  trimmings, for
  scrap packet
Flour, for dusting
Sugar, for sprinkling
Raspberry powder,
  for sprinkling
  (see Note on
  page 118)

Raspberry Twists

This is a fun way to use up your puff pastry scraps, and it's endlessly riffable! The raspberry powder is super tangy and adds a lovely acidic note against the sugar of the pastry. Don't want to buy raspberry powder? Cinnamon sugar is a tasty substitute! Want something savory instead of sweet? Nix the sugar and use shredded cheese!

Timeline

DAY ONE Making the scrap packet (5 minutes, plus one hour for resting), shaping pastries (20 minutes), baking pastries (30 minutes)

Prepare the scrap packet as described on page 24. Let it chill, wrapped in plastic, in the fridge for at least 1 hour and up to 1 day. Once it has relaxed, lightly dust a surface with flour and place the unwrapped packet on it. Lightly dust the top of the packet with flour as well, and begin rolling it out into a 12-inch-wide rectangle with ¼-inch thickness. The length will depend upon how much scrap you're working with. If the packet starts to stick to the surface or your rolling pin at any point, add some more flour to prevent that.

Once the dough is rolled out, make a mixture of sugar and raspberry powder in a small bowl. I like to use a ratio of 10 to 1 sugar to raspberry powder. So if you have 100 grams of sugar, you'd add 10 grams of raspberry powder. Mix it up with your hands and then sprinkle it over the bottom half of the dough. Be generous here! You don't want to see too much dough beneath the sugar. Reserve some raspberry sugar for later. Now fold the top half of the dough over the bottom half to enclose the sugar. Trim off the right edge, then cut into 1-inch strips.

continued

Once they're all cut, take one and rotate it so it's lengthwise. Pinch the open ends together, and then take one end in each hand and roll them in opposite directions to create a spiral. Some of the sugar may fall out, and that's OK! Once it's rolled into a spiraled baton shape, place it on a parchment-lined baking sheet. When you've finished all of them, scoop up all the raspberry sugar that fell out while shaping, and sprinkle it over the tops of the batons. Refrigerate if they get warm at any point in this process.

Preheat the oven to 375 degrees F.

Spread the batons out at least 1 inch apart from each other, and bake for 30 minutes. Let cool for at least 5 minutes before tossing them in the reserved raspberry sugar, then enjoy!

NOTE You can find raspberry powder at ShopKarensNaturals.com, or you can make your own by dehydrating 1 cup or so of fresh raspberries, then running them through a blender and sifting out the seeds with a sieve.

CROISSANT

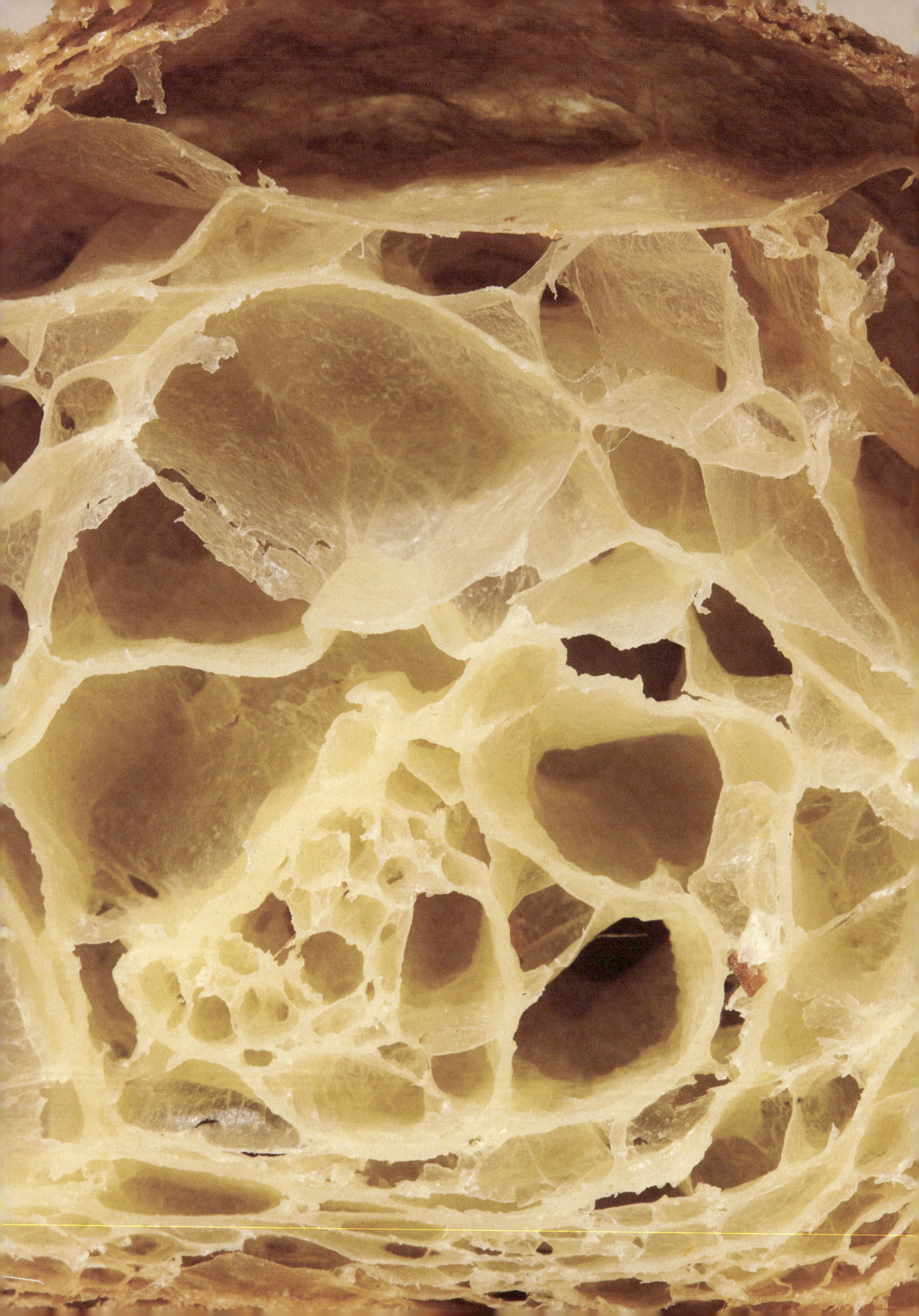

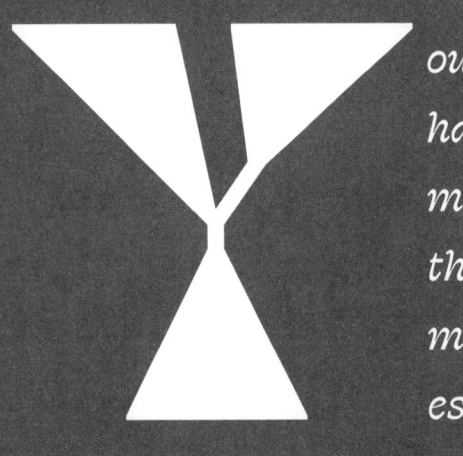ou should now be comfortable handling yeasted dough from making the brioche and with the laminating process from making the puff pastry—both essential skills you'll need to make croissants successfully. There are so many factors at play to create a successful croissant, so I will do my best to cover all aspects of them. First off, what makes a croissant successful? Here are my parameters: It has a slight crispness to its exterior, is soft on the inside, has distinguishable layers, has a honeycomb crumb structure inside, and flakes into a billion shards when you bite into it.

Mixing

First let's talk about the dough. Croissant dough is stiff, although not as stiff as puff pastry dough. It's important to keep the hydration low so when you laminate it, the dough isn't sliding off the butter block, which can happen if the dough is too soft (a.k.a too hydrated) when it's cold. The low hydration also helps with the crisp factor of the final pastry. You'll notice that the dough is slightly more enriched than puff pastry dough, including milk with the water for hydration. This will make the dough slightly more tender than puff pastry. This is key because the layers we create in croissant pastry will be slightly thicker than puff, and you'll want a more tender dough for a more pleasing mouthfeel.

When mixing this dough, the main goal is to develop enough gluten while keeping the dough cold to prevent fermentation. For this reason, I use ice water and cold ingredients, and I mix everything on low speed. It is important to run the mixer on low speed because we want to keep the dough very cold; since it has a long fermentation time in the fridge, we want to avoid the yeast from becoming too active, which would slow proofing down. It is also important to develop gluten to a moderate degree. I don't develop the gluten all the way because as it rests in the fridge overnight, and as we roll it out in the lamination process, it will continue to build strength, and I don't want to risk getting my dough hot from an extended mix time.

When it is done mixing, you should be left with a dough that is easily rolled on the table to be smooth on the outside, although it may not be smooth in the mixer. You'll want to immediately refrigerate the dough to keep it cold, and let the overnight fermentation work its magic.

Laminating

The lamination process will be similar to, but not quite the same as, the puff pastry. This dough will be a lot easier to roll out, and you'll be performing fewer turns, so I think it's a little easier to laminate personally. As long as you focus on creating even layers of dough/butter/dough when you lock in the butter and roll it out evenly, you should glide through lamination with ease.

Shaping

Shaping classic croissant shapes by hand can be tricky. As with the puff pastry, the dough will hold on to a lot of tension while you laminate, but because the dough is yeasted, you can't let it rest on the counter to let it relax. So instead of waiting to cut the dough, you'll do that right away, and then let the pieces rest in the fridge for at least 30 minutes before rolling them up. This method only applies to the classic croissant shape; cut-outs and chocolate croissants do not need this resting period. Never fight your dough; you will get frustrated, and you'll also probably lose! Patience and understanding are key here.

Proofing

A proper proof on croissants is paramount to their final outcome, and they are more temperamental than brioche. To preserve the layers that you so carefully and painstakingly created during lamination, you must not let the proofing temperature exceed 82 degrees F. If you do, the butter layers will begin to melt into the dough and muddy the honeycomb structure you're after. Underproofing croissants will result in massive amounts of butter leaking out of the pastries in the oven, and your croissants will be greasy on the bottom, not very large, and quite dense. Overproofing croissants will mean they don't get a lot of lift in the oven, and they will come out flat and too soft inside. A proper proof takes 2½ to 3 hours at 80 degrees F; your pastries will be almost tripled in size, and classic shapes will jiggle like Jello when the baking sheet is shaken. For cutouts, a good way to tell when they are properly proofed is when the layers begin to separate from each other.

For the biga
226 grams flour
187 grams water,
   at 70 degrees F
Very small pinch
   of yeast
Oil, for greasing

For the dough
188 grams cold water
153 grams milk
644 grams flour, plus
   more for dusting
88 grams sugar
21 grams butter, cold
21 grams salt
13 grams yeast

For the butter block
500 grams
   high-quality,
   low-moisture,
   unsalted,
   European-style
   butter

For the egg wash
1 egg yolk
2 tablespoons heavy
   cream or milk

PILLAR CROISSANT

Whenever I visit a bakery that's not my own, I always order a classic croissant. This is the benchmark against which I judge all other pastries; it's easy to make a Danish delicious because you have lots of other components to hide behind, but a classic croissant leaves no room for error. What am I looking for? I want to see a tall golden-brown pastry, not flat or pale or too dark. I want the outside to be crisp with an audible crunch on the first bite. The inside should have a honeycomb structure with lots of air pockets that are roughly the same size throughout. And it should taste like really good French butter! If it meets these criteria, I'm happy, but an added bonus is when the actual dough has a distinct and pleasing taste. Croissants should always start with a portion of the dough fermented before mixing the dough. This is essential to get a really good flavor in the dough itself. At my bakery, we make a sourdough preferment, but at home, it is more realistic to create a biga, which is basically a stiff yeasted dough.

Special equipment

Yardstick, ruler

Timeline

DAY ONE mixing biga (5 minutes), fermenting biga (12 to 14 hours)

DAY TWO mixing dough (25 minutes), fermenting dough (12 to 16 hours), making butter block (20 minutes)

DAY THREE laminating dough (2 hours), shaping dough (30 minutes, plus 30 minutes to rest), proofing dough (2 to 3 hours), baking croissants (25 to 30 minutes)

continued

MAKE THE BIGA Mix the flour, water, and yeast together, either in a mixer or by hand with a wooden spoon, to create a homogenous dough with no dry pockets of flour. There's no need to develop any gluten; you're simply mixing to disperse the water evenly throughout the flour.

Place in a lightly oiled bowl at least twice the size of the dough, cover in plastic wrap, and let sit at room temperature for 12 to 14 hours or until roughly doubled in size and poofy to the touch.

MAKE THE DOUGH Place the cold water, milk, flour, sugar, butter, salt, and yeast in a stand mixer fitted with the hook attachment. Add in all the mature biga. Mix on low speed for 25 minutes. If the dough climbs up the hook, simply stop the mixer, scrape it down, and begin mixing again. The dough should be somewhat smooth, although it may still have a few craggy pockets.

Roll this moderately developed dough into an egg shape, place on a parchment-lined baking sheet, and wrap the whole sheet with plastic. Even though the dough is cold, the yeast will still show some activity during the overnight cold fermentation and will likely nearly double in size. Put it in the fridge and let it ferment for at least 12 hours and up to 16.

LOCK IN THE BUTTER AND LAMINATE Make the butter block as described on page 16.

Depending on the ambient temperature of your kitchen, pull the butter block out of the refrigerator 30 minutes to 1 hour before you want to laminate. Keep an eye on its consistency, making sure it doesn't get too soft. It should be cold but flexible and should be of similar texture to the croissant dough. Try folding it slightly; if it breaks, it's too cold, and if your fingers squish it just by holding it, it's too warm. If you can bend it without breaking it and your fingers don't make any indentations on it, that's what you're looking for.

Take the croissant dough out of the fridge and transfer it to a lightly floured surface. Orient the egg so that its short side is toward you (photo 1). De-gas the dough by pushing your rolling pin into the center; repeat pressing it into the dough, moving from the center toward the edges (photo 2). Then roll it out to create a flat rectangle. There should be no large air bubbles in the dough. Roll the dough into a 21-by-7-inch rectangle of even thickness. Please note: The dimensions I took may differ slightly for you. The main things to focus on are keeping the dough of even thickness in each step and trying to achieve a rectangular shape that is rolled out thinly enough.

Rotate the dough so its long side is toward you. Visually divide the dough into four pieces and place the butter block in the middle two sections (photo 3). Fold the left flap over the top of the butter; it should

continued

land at the center line of the butter (photo 4). Make sure the dough is hugging the butter quite tightly at the point where it folds over. Press gently but firmly on the corners of the dough to secure it to the butter. Now do the same with the right flap of dough, having the two dough flaps meet each other in the center of the butter (photo 5).

This is called locking in the butter. What you're looking for here is an even thickness of dough all the way around an even layer of butter. When you look at this dough block from the side, you should see layers of dough/butter/dough that are all the same size (photo 6). The more fastidious you are about making these layers perfectly even and symmetrical, the easier the rest of the process will be, but you must not fuss over it too much or the warmth from your hands and the air will make the butter get too soft. If you don't achieve perfection on the first try, just know this is something I still work on with my own lamination, so don't be discouraged!

PERFORM A LETTER FOLD Now with the seam in the dough going perpendicular to you, start rolling the dough to lengthen it. You will only want to roll up and down, not sideways or diagonally; you're just lengthening it, not widening it. Roll it to ⅓-inch thick, which should give you a 25-by-11-inch rectangle. If the top and bottom of the rectangle are not straight sides, use a paring knife to trim the edges so you end up with a rectangle shape. Do not trim the long sides of the rectangle. Rotate the dough 90 degrees so the long side is toward you and perform a letter fold as described on page 20. Place on a baking sheet, wrap with plastic, and refrigerate for 30 minutes.

PERFORM A BOOK FOLD Take the dough out and place on a lightly floured surface, orienting the spine of the dough block to be on your left. Now you'll roll this out to ⅓-inch thickness, lengthening it only, ending up with a 30-by-8½-inch rectangle. Trim the short ends if necessary to make a nice rectangle, then perform a book fold as described on page 19. That's it! You're done laminating! Wrap it up in plastic and let it chill in the fridge for at least 1 hour before rolling it out to shape.

SHAPE, PROOF, AND BAKE After rolling the dough out to shape (see Shaping Classic Croissants, page 132), proof the pastries as described on page 125.

Preheat the oven to 350 degrees F.

Egg wash the croissants according to instructions on page 23 and pop them in the center of the oven for 25 to 30 minutes or until golden brown.

Shaping Classic Croissants

Roll the dough block out. If you get to a point in rolling out where it seems like the dough isn't getting any thinner and keeps springing back on you, transfer it to a baking sheet and pop it in the fridge for 10 minutes. Resting it will let the dough relax a little bit and rolling it will be easier.

You'll want to roll the dough block into a 32-by-13-inch rectangle that's a little less than ¼ inch thick. Once you have that, orient the dough so its long side is toward you. Take your yardstick and lay it across the bottom of the dough. Putting even pressure on it, use it as a guide to trim off a little strip from the bottom of the dough. Do the same at the top to achieve a dough that is exactly 12 inches wide. Now, starting from the right side of the dough, cut the curved part of the dough off to create a perfect rectangle shape. Place the beginning of the yardstick at the bottom right corner and make a small mark every 3½ inches. Place the ruler at the top right corner, measure 1¾ inches from that corner, then move the yardstick's beginning to that first mark and mark every 3½ inches from that.

Align the ruler with the 1¾-inch mark and the bottom right corner of the dough.

Cut on this angle. Move the ruler to the next two marks and cut again (photo 1). Continue until you reach the end of the marks. You should now have several trapezoidal cutouts. Now line up the ruler to go from the top right to the bottom left of each of those trapezoids and cut them in half. This will result in triangles (photo 2). You should have about 15 of them. Put them on a baking sheet, lightly cover with plastic wrap, and let rest in the fridge for 30 minutes.

Prepare the baking sheet with ungreased parchment paper. Take one triangle and gently stretch it to lengthen it by about 1 or 2 inches. With the bottom of the triangle toward you, start rolling the pastry up away from you (photos 3 to 6). Make sure the tail end of it is directly underneath the rolled-up pastry so it doesn't open up in the oven. Voilà, you've shaped a croissant!

Continue with the remaining pastries. Put up to six on that parchment-lined baking sheet. You can freeze them for later use (see Note) or you can proof them right away.

NOTE When freezing, make sure they are separate from each other so they don't stick together, which could tear the layers apart when separating later. To thaw, simply put them in the refrigerator overnight. Proofing may take slightly longer (up to 3½ hours at 80 degrees F) if working from thawed pastry rather than fresh. You can freeze pastries for up to 3 weeks.

1 recipe Pillar
 Croissant (page 127)
Flour, for dusting
100 grams
 Emmentaler,
 Gruyère, or Swiss
 cheese, shredded

For the filling
250 grams pancetta,
 cut into ½-inch
 cubes
1 large bunch curly
 kale, destemmed
 and torn into large
 pieces
Salt and freshly
 ground black
 pepper

For the custard
150 grams large eggs
 (about 3 eggs)
3 egg yolks
360 grams half-
 and-half
½ teaspoon salt
¼ teaspoon freshly
 ground black
 pepper
Pinch of nutmeg

Kale-Pancetta Croissant Quiche

I had all but given up on quiche until I worked at a bakery in Seattle that changed my mind on it forever. I was so tired of overcooked eggs and soggy pie dough, so when I had a slice of a quiche made with croissant dough, it was a paradigm shift for me. Once you try this, you'll never go back to pie-crust quiche again! Crisp, salty pancetta cubes and leafy kale provide a lot of flavor and texture against this super rich and soft egg custard.

Special equipment

9-inch pie dish, cheese grater, immersion blender (optional), strainer

Timeline

DAY ONE mixing biga (5 minutes), fermenting biga (overnight)

DAY TWO mixing dough (25 minutes), fermenting dough (12 to 16 hours), making butter block (20 minutes)

DAY THREE laminating dough (2 hours), shaping dough (30 minutes), making filling (30 minutes), baking pastry (1 hour)

Follow the steps in Pillar Croissant recipe through laminating. Roll out the dough to ⅛-inch thickness and cut an 11-inch circle out of it. Place it on a lightly floured baking sheet, cover in plastic wrap, and put in the fridge to stay cold while you make the filling. Save any remaining dough for another use.

continued

MAKE THE FILLING Add the pancetta to a cold medium skillet and set over medium heat. Cook, stirring occasionally, until the fat has rendered out and the pancetta is crispy. Transfer the pancetta to a paper towel-lined plate to drain, reserving the fat in the pan. Add half the kale to the pan, stirring to coat in oil until wilted. Add the other half of the kale and repeat. Season with salt and pepper, remembering that the pancetta is salty on its own, so taste before adding more. Cook until the kale has released a lot of its water and the pan is dry, about 5 minutes. Transfer to a plate to let cool.

MAKE THE CUSTARD Add the eggs, yolks, and half-and-half to a bowl. Whisk or immersion blend until smooth. Run it through a strainer and then whisk in the salt, pepper, and nutmeg.

There is no need to proof this pastry! Drape the croissant round over the top of a 9-inch pie dish. Gently push the dough down to the bottom and along the sides of the dish. There will be excess dough along the sides of the dish; decoratively fold that excess dough on top of itself in six to eight areas to make it fit snugly into the dish. If the dough starts to get warm at all, put it in the fridge for 10 minutes.

Preheat the oven to 350 degrees F.

Toss the now completely cooled kale and pancetta together, transfer to the shell, and then pour the custard over it. Top with the shredded cheese and bake for 1 hour or until the crust is golden brown, the cheese has taken on some dark spots, and the custard is just set in the center. It will soufflé gently.

Serve warm or at room temperature. Or eat a slice straight from the fridge after a long day at work. This will keep in the fridge, wrapped in plastic, for up to 4 days.

For the dough
1 recipe Pillar
  Croissant (page 127)
Flour, for dusting

For the béchamel
370 grams whole milk
30 grams butter
15 grams flour
Pinch of nutmeg
Salt and pepper

For the filling
6 tablespoons olive
  oil
1½ pounds mixed
  mushrooms, such as
  shiitake, chanterelle,
  maitake, or lion's
  mane, cut in ½-inch
  slices
Salt
3 tablespoons butter
2 sprigs of thyme
3 garlic cloves,
  crushed
3 tablespoons red
  wine vinegar
200 grams Comté
  cheese, shredded

Wild Mushroom and Comté Croissant

Yet another wow factor of the Pacific Northwest for me was the abundance of mushrooms! So many varieties, such different textures, and you can buy them wild foraged at the farmers' markets. Use a variety of mushrooms for these pastries to get the best results; just make sure to cut or tear them into same-size pieces so they cook at the same rate. The most important aspect of cooking mushrooms for pastries is to get as much of the water out as you can before putting them in the oven and then getting a nice crispy crust on them. To do that, you'll use high heat to sear them, then baste them in butter after they've released their liquid. Hit with a little acid at the end, and they're divine!

Special equipment

4-inch circle cookie cutter

Timeline

DAY ONE mixing biga (5 minutes), fermenting biga (12 to 14 hours)

DAY TWO mixing dough (25 minutes), fermenting dough and making béchamel (12 to 16 hours), making butter block (20 minutes)

DAY THREE laminating dough (2 hours), shaping dough (30 minutes), making filling (30 minutes), proofing dough (2 to 3 hours), baking pastries (30 minutes)

MAKE THE DOUGH: Follow the steps in Pillar Croissant recipe through laminating.

MAKE THE BÉCHAMEL: While your dough in the Pillar Croissant recipe is fermenting, make the béchamel so it can cool overnight in tandem. Heat the milk in a small pot over low heat until steaming. Simultaneously, in a small saucepan, melt the butter over medium heat. Once the butter stops foaming, whisk in the flour to create

continued

a roux. Continue to cook, whisking occasionally, for 1 to 2 minutes or until the flour turns a golden color and the raw taste has been cooked out. Add the hot milk to the roux in a slow, steady stream, whisking constantly to prevent clumping. Cook, whisking often, until it thickens. Add a pinch of nutmeg and season to taste with salt and pepper. Transfer to a container, pressing plastic wrap onto the surface to prevent a skin from forming, and refrigerate overnight or until completely cooled.

SHAPE THE DOUGH Roll out the dough to ¼-inch thickness and use a 4-inch cookie cutter to cut circles out of it. Place them on a lightly floured baking sheet, cover in plastic wrap, and put in the fridge to stay cold while you make the filling.

MAKE THE FILLING Heat the olive oil in a 12-inch skillet over medium-high heat until shimmering. Add the mushrooms and let cook undisturbed for 3 to 5 minutes or until they are golden brown. Add salt to taste and continue to cook, stirring occasionally, until the mushrooms have released some liquid and that has evaporated, 8 to 10 minutes. Once the skillet looks dry, add the butter, thyme, and garlic. Stir constantly to baste the mushrooms in the butter and aromatics, until the garlic is golden and everything is smelling way too good. Turn the heat off and add the vinegar. Season with salt and transfer to a plate to cool.

Place the rounds of croissant dough onto a parchment-lined baking sheet. You can fit up to six on a baking sheet. Proof the pastries as described on page 125. For flat cutouts of croissants, as opposed to the classic croissant shape, proofing is evident when the layers begin to separate from themselves, and it generally doesn't take as long. Check on them at 1½ hours.

Preheat the oven to 350 degrees F.

Spread about 1 tablespoon of the béchamel into the center of each round of dough, leaving about a ½ inch of border around the perimeter. Gently push about 3 tablespoons of mushrooms over the béchamel. It's OK to deflate the center of the dough a little here; it will help the filling stay in place in the oven. Top each with a generous pile of Comté. Transfer to the center of the oven and bake for 28 to 30 minutes or until the cheese is bubbling and getting a little color. Serve warm.

**Makes 15 to
18 croissants**

1 recipe Pillar
  Croissant (page 127)
Flour, for dusting

*For the roasted
strawberries*
1 kilogram
  strawberries, hulled
  (about 2¼ pounds)
100 grams sugar
10 grams sumac

*For the cheesecake
mousse*
400 grams cream
  cheese, at room
  temperature
112 grams sugar
½ vanilla bean,
  seeds scraped, or
  ½ teaspoon vanilla
  extract
168 grams high–
  quality white
  chocolate
228 grams heavy
  cream

For the egg wash
1 egg yolk
2 tablespoons heavy
  cream or milk

Sumac-Roasted Strawberry Cheesecake Croissant

This recipe is great for the months when strawberries are not at their peak. Roasting them will concentrate their sweetness and make even the most lackluster berries shine. I've added sumac to them, a sour Middle Eastern spice that plays off the sweetness of the berries. The cheesecake mousse puts this pastry over the top, the creaminess a perfect complement to the pastry's flakiness and crisp.

Special equipment

Teardrop cookie cutter or 4-inch circle cookie cutter, piping bag with big star tip

Timeline

DAY ONE mixing biga (5 minutes), fermenting biga (12 to 14 hours)

DAY TWO mixing dough (25 minutes), fermenting dough (12 to 16 hours), making butter block (20 minutes)

DAY THREE laminating dough (2 hours), shaping dough (30 minutes), proofing dough (2 to 3 hours), roasting strawberries (30 minutes), making cheesecake mousse (20 minutes), baking croissants (30 minutes), filling croissants (10 minutes)

Follow the steps in Pillar Croissant recipe through laminating. Roll out the dough to ¼-inch thickness and cut the pastry; I use a teardrop-shaped cookie cutter for this, but you can use a 4-inch circle cutter as well. Place the dough onto a lightly floured surface, and use the cutter to punch out discs of dough. Put them on a parchment-lined baking sheet. (For any dough you don't want to bake the same day, you can freeze it, tightly double-wrapped in plastic, for up to 1 month.)

continued

Proof the dough as described on page 125. For flat cutouts of croissants, as opposed to the classic croissant shape, proofing is evident when the layers begin to separate from themselves, and it generally doesn't take as long. Start checking on them at 1½ hours.

While the pastries are proofing, make the roasted strawberries: Preheat the oven to 375 degrees F. Cut large berries in half. In a large bowl, toss the strawberries with the sugar and sumac, and place on a parchment-lined baking sheet. Roast in the center of the oven for 30 minutes, stirring every 10 minutes, until the berries are tender but still hold their shape. There should not be any runny liquid on the pan. Set them aside in a bowl.

MAKE THE CHEESECAKE MOUSSE In the bowl of a stand mixer fitted with the paddle attachment, mix the cream cheese, sugar, and vanilla on medium-low speed.

Meanwhile, melt the white chocolate in the microwave in 20-second increments, stirring well between each heating. With the mixer running, pour the melted white chocolate into the cream cheese mixture in a slow, steady stream. Once it is fully incorporated, stop the mixer.

In a separate bowl, whip the cream to medium stiff peaks. With a spatula, fold the whipped cream into the cheesecake mixture. This may prove to be a little difficult as the cream cheese is going to be a lot stiffer than the whipped cream. Don't worry too much about deflating the whipped cream; just get it incorporated in as few movements as possible. Refrigerate until ready to use.

Preheat the oven to 350 degrees F.

Brush the tops of the pastries with egg wash (see instructions on page 23).

Carefully place about 2 tablespoons of the roasted strawberries into the center of each pastry, leaving a ½-inch border around the perimeter. No need to press these down, as the liquid released during baking will prevent the pastry from pushing the filling up.

Bake for 25 to 30 minutes or until the pastry is golden brown. Let cool completely.

Fit the piping bag with a large star tip, and fill it with the cheesecake mousse. Pipe a swirl on top of the pastry to fully cover the strawberries. Serve immediately.

Mapo Tofu Pot Pie

1 recipe Pillar
  Croissant (page 127)
Flour, for dusting

For the filling
4 to 8 grams
  whole Sichuan
  peppercorns,
  depending on how
  numbing you like it
56 grams
  vegetable oil
36 grams
  minced ginger
36 grams
  minced garlic
380 grams
  ground pork
40 to 60 grams
  doubanjiang
  (see Note on
  page 144)
½ cup mushroom
  stock or water
6 grams cornstarch
56 grams water
1 pound soft tofu,
  drained and sliced
  into 1-inch cubes
¼ teaspoon
  sesame oil
56 grams chili oil
2 scallions,
  finely sliced
Salt

For the egg wash
1 egg yolk
2 tablespoons heavy
  cream or milk

When I lived in Gainesville, there was a woman named Jenny,
originally from Singapore, who ran a booth at the farmers'
market. She owned a fruit orchard specializing in blueberries
and chestnuts, but she also made curry pot pies to sell alongside her produce. They were little bowls filled with simple
Singaporean curry with potatoes, veggies, and chicken, and
topped with a round of pie crust; something that was at once
comforting and novel. This recipe is an ode to that dish, and
to that sweet woman. If you're vegetarian, swap out the pork
for mushrooms.

Special equipment

10-ounce ramekins or similar individual-sized baking vessels, circle
cookie cutter 1 inch larger than the baking vessels, mortar and pestle
or spice grinder

Timeline

DAY ONE mixing biga (5 minutes), fermenting biga (12 to 14 hours)

DAY TWO mixing dough (25 minutes), fermenting dough (12 to
16 hours), making butter block (20 minutes)

DAY THREE laminating dough (2 hours), making filling (30 minutes),
proofing pot pies (30 minutes), baking pot pies (28 to 30 minutes)

Follow the steps in Pillar Croissant recipe through laminating. Roll out
the dough to ⅛-inch thickness and cut out four circles with a diameter
1 inch larger than the baking vessels. Place on a lightly floured baking
sheet, cover in plastic wrap, and put in the fridge to stay cold while
you make the filling.

continued

Mapo Tofu Pot Pie, continued

MAKE THE FILLING Grind the peppercorns in a mortar and pestle or spice grinder until coarsely ground, and set aside. Heat the vegetable oil in a skillet over medium heat until shimmering. Add the ginger and cook for 1 minute, then add the garlic. Continue to cook until fragrant, about 30 seconds, taking care not to burn the garlic. Turn the heat up to medium high and add the pork. Break it up with a wooden spoon until crumbly and cooked through. Add the ground pepper and stir to combine. Add the doubanjiang and stir. Once combined, add the mushroom stock and simmer for about 1 minute.

Meanwhile, whisk together the cornstarch and 56 grams of water in a small bowl to create a slurry. Once the pork has simmered for about 1 minute, stir in the slurry and continue to simmer until it thickens slightly. Add the tofu, sesame oil, chili oil, and scallions, stirring very gently to keep the tofu intact. Let it simmer for about 5 minutes, reducing the heat if it starts boiling. Taste for seasoning and add salt if needed. Set aside and cool to room temperature.

Transfer the cooled filling into four ramekins. Put the ramekins on a baking sheet. Place a croissant dough circle on top of each ramekin, pressing gently but firmly to adhere the dough to the rim of the ramekins. Take the tip of a paring knife and create an X in the center of each one to let steam vent out.

Preheat the oven to 350 degrees F.

Proof the pot pies (see Proofing, page 125), lightly cover with plastic wrap, at room temperature for about 30 minutes. These don't take long to proof because they are so thin. You may not see much growth of the dough; that's OK!

Brush each lid with egg wash (see instructions on page 23) and bake for 28 to 30 minutes or until the pastry is golden brown and the filling is bubbling. Let cool for 5 to 10 minutes before serving.

NOTE Doubanjiang, a fermented spicy bean sauce used as a foundation for mapo tofu, can be purchased from your local Asian market or online.

1 recipe Pillar
  Croissant (page 127)
Basil leaves, for
  garnishing

*For the blistered
tomatoes*
600 grams cherry
  tomatoes
  (about 2 pints)
3 tablespoons
  olive oil
Salt
Red pepper flakes

*For the cheese
mixture*
250 grams ricotta
100 grams shredded
  fontina
100 grams shredded
  mozzarella
50 grams grated
  Parmesan
4 grams salt
2 grams freshly
  ground black
  pepper
100 grams heavy
  cream

For the egg wash
1 egg yolk
2 tablespoons heavy
  cream or milk

Cheesy Blistered Tomato Croissant

There are some fundamental rules to follow for creating pastry filling combinations. First, the filling should not have too much water content in it because water leakage on a pastry will make it a soggy mess. This is why you'll blister these tomatoes before baking them on the pastry, as it not only concentrates their flavor but also reduces their sog factor. Second, cheese is always the right answer! Not only is it delicious, it is also going to act as a barrier against any extra moisture those tomatoes might be holding on to. You'll end up with a pastry that's crisp and flaky on the bottom, sweet and jammy in the middle, and topped with cheesy goodness.

Timeline

DAY ONE mixing biga (5 minutes), fermenting biga (12 to 14 hours)

DAY TWO mixing dough (25 minutes), fermenting dough (12 to 16 hours), making butter block (20 minutes)

DAY THREE laminating dough (2 hours), blistering tomatoes (5 to 6 minutes), shaping dough (30 minutes), making cheese mixture (30 minutes), proofing dough (2 to 3 hours), baking pastries (25 to 30 minutes)

Follow the steps in Pillar Croissant recipe through laminating.

MAKE THE BLISTERED TOMATOES Position a rack in the oven close to the broiler element. Turn the broiler on high.

In a large bowl, toss the tomatoes with olive oil and season to taste with salt and red pepper flakes. Pour the tomatoes out onto a rimmed baking sheet lined with aluminum foil and broil for 5 to 6 minutes, shaking the pan halfway through. You're looking for some black spots to appear on the skins. Let cool completely and drain off any liquid that has collected.

continued

Roll out the dough to ¼ inch thick. Using a ruler and a sharp knife, cut the dough into 4½-inch squares. Keep the pastry squares you want to bake refrigerated while you make the cheese mixture. Any unused pastry dough can be frozen tightly wrapped in plastic for up to 1 month for later use.

MAKE THE CHEESE MIXTURE Combine all cheeses, the salt, and pepper in a large bowl and stir to combine. Add cream and stir to combine.

Place up to six pastry squares on a parchment-lined baking sheet. Carefully spread 2 to 3 tablespoons of the cheese mixture into the middle of the pastries, leaving a 1-inch border around the edges.

Proof as described on page 125.

Preheat the oven to 350 degrees F.

When the pastries are proofed, gently egg wash according to instructions on page 23, and top each pastry with enough tomatoes to cover most of the cheese. Press down slightly here to make sure the pastry doesn't pop up and push the tomatoes off in the oven. Bake for 25 to 30 minutes or until the pastries are golden brown and the cheese is bubbling.

Garnish with torn basil leaves and serve.

For the biga
226 grams flour
187 grams water
Very small pinch
  of yeast
Oil, for greasing

*For the chocolate
croissant dough*
500 grams
  European-style
  butter, for the
  butter block
188 grams cold water
153 grams milk
644 grams flour
187 grams water
88 grams sugar
25 grams brute
  cocoa powder
21 grams butter, cold
21 grams salt
13 grams yeast
30 grams dark
  chocolate, melted

*For the chocolate
whipped ganache*
3 grams sheet gelatin
Cold water, for
  blooming
392 grams heavy
  cream, divided
88 grams high–
  quality milk
  chocolate, chopped

For the egg wash
1 egg yolk
2 tablespoons heavy
  cream or milk
Mini chocolate chips,
  for sprinkling

Triple Chocolate Croissant

I've never cared for a traditional pain au chocolat. I'm too in love with chocolate to have just a little slab of it in the center of an otherwise plain croissant! This recipe is for serious chocolate lovers, as it includes chocolate in the dough itself, has mini chocolate chips throughout the pastry, and is then filled with a whipped chocolate ganache post-bake.

Special equipment

Immersion blender, piping bag

Timeline

DAY ONE mixing biga (5 minutes), fermenting biga (12 to 14 hours)

DAY TWO making butter block (20 minutes), mixing dough (25 minutes), fermenting dough (12 to 16 hours)

DAY THREE laminating dough (2 hours), making chocolate whipped ganache (20 minutes), shaping dough (30 minutes), proofing dough (2 to 3 hours), baking croissants (27 to 30 minutes), filling croissants (5 minutes)

MAKE THE BIGA Two days before you want to eat the croissants, mix the flour, the water, and the yeast together until homogenous. Let it ferment in a covered lightly oiled bowl at room temperature for 12 to 14 hours.

MAKE THE CHOCOLATE CROISSANT DOUGH Make the butter block as described on page 16.

Place the cold water, milk, flour, sugar, cocoa powder, butter, salt, and yeast in a stand mixer fitted with the hook attachment. Add in all the biga and melted chocolate, and start the mixer right away so the chocolate doesn't have time to solidify. Using this dough, follow the steps in Pillar Croissant recipe (page 127) up to the lamination. The dough should be a light brown color without any visible chunks of chocolate after its rest.

continued

Laminate the dough as described on page 124.

MAKE THE CHOCOLATE WHIPPED GANACHE Bloom the gelatin in ice water. Meanwhile, heat 204 grams of the cream in a small saucepan over medium-high heat.

When the gelatin has bloomed, squeeze excess water out of it and put it in a heatproof bowl with the chocolate. When the cream comes to a boil, pour it over the chocolate and gelatin. Gently stir to melt the chocolate completely. Immersion blend this mixture to make sure it is homogenous, scraping the bottom and sides of the bowl to ensure there's no chocolate hiding there.

With the immersion blender running, stream in the remaining 188 grams of cream. Transfer this to a container and place plastic wrap directly on top of it to prevent any sweating. Refrigerate overnight.

Roll the laminated dough out to a 16-by-19-inch rectangle about ¼ inch thick. You're going to be cutting 7-by-3-inch rectangles out of this dough. To get the most out of this dough, trim the bottom edge using a ruler as a guide to keep it straight.

From that first cut, measure 7 inches up from it, make a little mark in the dough, and then measure 7 more inches from that mark. Do it again in a different spot on the dough so you have two points to cut along. Line the ruler up along the middle two marks (these are the ones 7 inches up from the bottom trim) and cut the dough lengthwise. Now do the same thing where the marks are 14 inches up from the bottom trim. This will leave you with two 7-inch-wide strips of dough.

You're going to do the same thing going crosswise now. Start at the right side of the strips. Trim an edge off. Now from that edge, make a mark every 3 inches. Cut crosswise at all the 3-inch marks. You should now have about twelve 7-by-3-inch rectangles.

Egg wash the pastry according to instructions on page 23, and sprinkle the chocolate chips all over the rectangles. To roll up the pastries, start with one of the short ends and start rolling it up like you would a cinnamon roll (photo 1). It's OK if some chocolate chips escape, just gather them up and push them back on unrolled pastries.

continued

You'll end up with a cylinder shape, and the seam should be on the bottom. Repeat this with all the rectangles.

If you don't want to bake all of them today, you can freeze some. Tightly wrap them in plastic and keep them frozen for up to 3 weeks.

Put up to six croissants on a parchment-lined baking sheet. Proof the pastries as described on page 125.

Preheat the oven to 350 degrees F.

Egg wash each pastry according to instructions on page 23. Bake in the center of the oven for 27 to 30 minutes. Let cool completely.

Once the pastries are cool, transfer the ganache into a stand mixer fitted with the whisk attachment. Whisk on medium-high speed until stiff peaks form. Transfer the whipped ganache to a piping bag. Fill the pastries as described on page 24. Serve immediately.

For the biga
226 grams flour
187 grams water
Very small pinch
  of yeast
Oil, for greasing

For the pandan
croissant dough
500 grams butter, for
  the butter block
188 grams cold water
153 grams milk
644 grams flour
187 grams water
88 grams sugar
21 grams butter, cold
21 grams salt
13 grams yeast
1 teaspoon pandan
  paste (see Note on
  page 156)

For the pandan
custard
460 grams milk
114 grams sugar,
  divided
75 grams egg yolks
40 grams cornstarch
30 grams butter
½ teaspoon pandan
  paste

For the egg wash
1 egg yolk
2 tablespoons heavy
  cream or milk

Pandan Custard Croissant

I first encountered pandan in the form of jelly candies from a Vietnamese bakery in Seattle. Pandan has a very subtle but pleasing flavor, like a vegetal vanilla-coconut hybrid. For this croissant recipe, you will be adding pandan paste to the croissant dough; everything else is exactly the same as the Pillar Croissant recipe (page 127). Once baked, the pandan croissants are filled with a pandan custard.

Special equipment

Piping bag

Timeline

DAY ONE mixing biga (5 minutes), fermenting biga (12 to 14 hours)

DAY TWO making butter block (20 minutes), mixing dough (25 minutes), fermenting dough (12 to 16 hours), making filling (20 minutes plus overnight to chill)

DAY THREE laminating dough (2 hours), shaping dough (30 minutes), making pandan custard (20 minutes), proofing dough (2 to 3 hours), baking croissants (25 to 30 minutes), filling croissants (5 minutes)

MAKE THE BIGA Two days before you want to eat croissants, mix the flour, the water, and the yeast together until homogenous. Let it ferment in a covered lightly oiled bowl at room temperature for 12 to 14 hours.

MAKE THE PANDAN CROISSANT DOUGH Make the butter block as described on page 16.

Place the cold water, milk, flour, sugar, butter, salt, and yeast in a stand mixer fitted with the hook attachment. Add in all the biga and pandan paste, and mix. Using this dough, follow the steps in Pillar Croissant recipe up to the lamination. The dough should be a light green color after its rest.

continued

Laminate the dough as described on page 124.

Shape as described on page 125.

MAKE THE PANDAN CUSTARD In a small saucepot, heat the milk and 57 grams of the sugar over medium–high heat.

In a medium heatproof bowl, whisk together the remaining 57 grams of sugar, the egg yolks, and cornstarch until homogenous. Set aside.

When the milk comes to a boil, take it off the heat and slowly stream it into the egg mixture in a slow, steady stream, whisking the entire time. Once about two-thirds of the milk is added to the egg mixture, put the pot back over medium heat and quickly add the hot egg/milk mixture back into the pot. Whisk constantly until the mixture thickens. Continue to cook, whisking constantly, for another 20 to 30 seconds to cook the cornstarch taste out of the custard.

Take off the heat, whisk in the butter and pandan paste, and transfer to a container. Put plastic wrap directly on top to prevent a skin from forming and cool in the refrigerator until set, at least 3 hours or up to overnight.

Place up to six croissants on a parchment-lined baking sheet. Proof the pastries as described on page 125.

Preheat the oven to 350 degrees F.

Egg wash according to instructions on page 23. Bake for 25 to 30 minutes or until the pastry is golden. Let cool completely.

Once the pastries are cool, transfer the pandan custard to a piping bag. Fill the pastries as described on page 24. Serve immediately.

NOTE You can find pandan paste online or at specialty Asian markets.

*For the five-spice
mixture*
75 grams sugar
8 grams Chinese
 five-spice powder
1 recipe Pillar
 Croissant (page 127)
Cold water, for
 brushing
200 grams sugar,
 plus more as
 needed

Chinese Five-Spice Kouign Amann

Kouign Amann has to be one of my all-time favorite pastries. It is essentially a croissant that is laminated with sugar *and* butter instead of just butter, then coated in sugar and baked. The sugar on the outside caramelizes and hardens to produce a thin, shattering lacquer; the sugar on the inside melts and becomes gooey, making an almost custard-like filling. When done right, they are perfection. I've added Chinese five-spice powder to the sugar mixture for a little added flair. You can leave it out if you want something more classic.

Special equipment

3½-inch ring molds or oversized muffin tins (see Note on page 162), spray bottle (optional)

Timeline

DAY ONE mixing biga (5 minutes), fermenting biga (12 to 14 hours)

DAY TWO mixing dough (25 minutes), fermenting dough (12 to 16 hours), making butter block (20 minutes)

DAY THREE laminating dough (2 hours), shaping dough (30 minutes), proofing dough (2 to 3 hours), baking pastries (27 to 30 minutes)

MAKE THE FIVE-SPICE MIXTURE Mix the sugar with the Chinese five-spice powder in a small bowl.

Follow the steps in Pillar Croissant recipe up to the first letter fold. The lamination on this pastry is a little bit different but really no more difficult than laminating croissants. Once you've locked in the butter and performed the first letter fold as described in the pillar recipe, you'll do another letter fold instead of doing a book fold.

Let that rest for 30 minutes, then roll it out to do yet another letter fold. But before you finalize the third fold, we'll add the five-spice mixture.

continued

MEASURE AND CUT THE DOUGH Visually divide the dough into thirds. Add half the five-spice mixture to the middle third of the dough, using your hand to spread it evenly all the way up to the edges (photo 1).

Fold the left third over the middle, and now cover the top half with the remaining five-spice mixture, again spreading it evenly all the way to the edges (photo 2).

Fold the right third over the middle. Now let that rest at least 1 hour in the refrigerator (photo 3).

To shape the pastries, roll the dough block out to a 10-by-32-inch rectangle. You're going to cut 4½-inch squares out of this.

Start by using a ruler to trim the bottom edge; discard the trimming. Now, measuring from that bottom edge, make a small mark in the dough 4½ inches up, 9 inches up, and 13½ inches up from the bottom. Repeat this again on a different part of the dough to make straight lines. Place the ruler on both of the marks that are 4½ inches up from the bottom and cut along the ruler (photo 4).

Repeat at both marks that are 9 inches up. You should now have two strips that are 4½ inches wide (photo 5). Now you're going to cut crosswise. Start from the right side of the strips and trim off an edge (photo 6). Measure from that edge at 4½, 9, 13½, 18, and 22½ inches, and so on as necessary. Cut along those marks to make the squares of dough. You should get 12 to 15 pieces (photos 7 and 8).

continued

SHAPE Brush both sides of every pastry piece with cold water or mist them with a spray bottle. Completely coat them by putting them in a pie dish filled with the sugar and tossing them around (photo 1). Add more sugar as needed. Place the squares in the fridge for 1 minute while you prep the baking molds by spraying them with pan spray. If using ring molds, place them on a parchment-lined baking sheet.

Bring one square out of the fridge at a time so the rest stay cold. Turn the square so it looks like a diamond on the counter in front of you. Fold each corner into the center of the pastry so it becomes a square (photos 2 and 3). Press all the tips down very firmly with your fingertip (you should be able to feel the countertop through the pastry if you're pressing hard enough). Don't go all the way through the pastry, but very nearly through it (photo 4).

NOW THE TRICKY PART Take your thumbs and forefingers and place one finger on each corner of the square you've now formed. Without undoing the center, push up and in toward the center with all four of your fingers at once (photos 5 to 8). You should end up with a four-leaf clover type of shape. Plop that into a prepared baking mold and repeat with the others.

Proof the pastries as described on page 125. You cannot freeze any of the unused ones as the sugar in between the layers of the dough will start eating away at it. You can, however, keep the squares refrigerated for up to 24 hours before shaping them.

Preheat the oven to 350 degrees F.

No need to egg wash these. Bake them in the center of the oven for 27 to 30 minutes or until the tops are darkly caramelized. Immediately remove them from their baking molds and let them cool on a baking sheet without parchment paper. Once the caramel has hardened, you can enjoy them. If you have leftovers, they make excellent vehicles for ice cream sandwiches!

NOTE I like to use bottomless stainless steel cake rings for these pastries so any extra butter or caramel can leak out the bottom and not make the pastries greasy. If you don't have these, an oversized muffin tin will work. If you're using stainless steel, make sure to generously spray the rings with nonstick cooking spray and put them on a parchment-lined baking sheet (up to 6 per sheet). If you're using a nonstick muffin pan, no need to spray it.

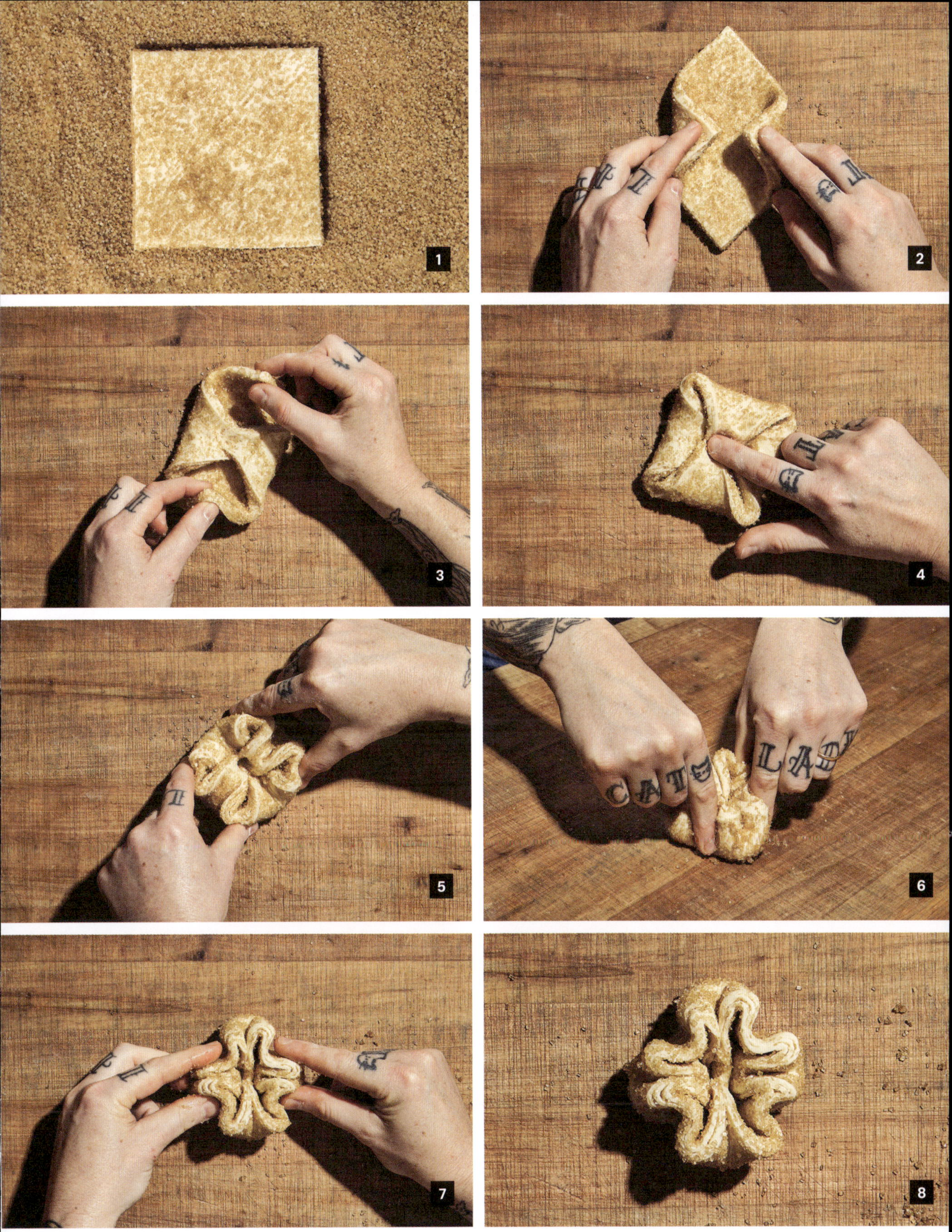
1
2
3
4
5
6
7
8

Spiced Date Scrolls

with Labneh Glaze

Makes about 6 to 15 scrolls, depending on how much croissant dough scrap you have

For the date paste
500 grams dried and pitted Medjool dates
5 grams ground cinnamon
2 grams ground nutmeg

For the labneh glaze
450 grams powdered sugar
125 grams labneh or plain whole milk Greek yogurt
½ teaspoon vanilla extract
Scraps and trimmings from croissant dough, for scrap packet
Flour, for dusting
Cinnamon, for dusting (optional)

These are a variation on date and almond scrolls, something we use croissant scraps for at Temple Pastries, except this glaze includes labneh, a Mediterranean strained yogurt. The tanginess of the glaze helps balance out the dates' natural sweetness. If you can't find labneh, use a plain, whole fat Greek yogurt in its place.

Special equipment

Food processor, offset spatula

Timeline

DAY ONE making scrap packet (5 minutes plus at least one hour for chilling), making the date paste (15 minutes), making the labneh glaze (5 minutes), shaping the pastries (10 minutes), proofing the pastries (2 to 3 hours), baking the pastries (25 to 30 minutes), glazing the pastries (5 minutes)

MAKE THE DATE PASTE Place the dates in a heatproof bowl. Bring a small pot of water to a boil and pour the hot water over the dates. Let it sit for 10 minutes, then drain off the water, reserving it. Feel around in each date to make sure there are no stray pits. This is easier to do after they've soaked in the hot water. Put the dates and spices in a food processor and turn it on. Add the soaking water 1 tablespoon at a time, until the mixture is able to churn into a paste. Transfer to a bowl. You can keep this refrigerated in a lidded container for up to 1 month.

MAKE THE LABNEH GLAZE Whisk the powdered sugar, labneh, and vanilla together until smooth. This can be stored in the refrigerator for up to 1 month.

continued

Prepare the scrap packet as described on page 24. Let it chill for at least 1 hour or up to 1 day, wrapped in plastic in the fridge. Once it has relaxed, lightly dust a surface with flour and place the unwrapped packet on it. Lightly dust the top of the packet as well, and begin rolling it out into a rectangle that has a 15-inch width and ¼-inch thickness. The length will depend upon how much scrap you're working with. If the packet starts to stick to the surface or your rolling pin at any point, add some more flour to prevent that.

Once the packet is rolled out, use a small offset spatula to spread a thin layer of date paste all over the dough, leaving the bottom inch bare along the side closest to you. Starting from the side farthest away from you, start rolling the dough up like a cinnamon roll. Trim the butt end off and discard.

Then cut the log every inch to create the scrolls. Using a very sharp chef's knife in two decisive motions is the best way to get a clean cut, but you can also use a serrated knife.

Set the pastry on a parchment-lined baking sheet so the swirl faces up, and tuck the loose end underneath. Repeat with remaining pastries, and proof as described on page 125.

Preheat the oven to 350 degrees F.

Bake in the center of the oven for 25 to 30 minutes or until just golden. While the pastries are still hot, brush them with a generous amount of the labneh glaze, and dust with more cinnamon if desired. Let cool for about 10 minutes and then enjoy!

Troubleshooting

Brioche

The Dough Breaks before Done Mixing
This is a result of gluten forming and then breaking down from overmixing. Try adding the butter earlier in the mixing process, making sure the butter is room temperature before adding it.

The Brioche Tastes Dry and Eggy
This happens when the butter is not emulsified properly in the dough. There are two things that can cause this: The dough temperature was too hot when butter was added during the mix or the temperature for proofing was too warm. If you suspect the first cause, try chilling all the ingredients (minus the butter) in the freezer for 30 minutes before mixing. You can also try chilling the mixing bowl. If you suspect the second cause, keep a closer eye on the proofing environment and make sure it stays below 82 degrees F.

The Brioche Tears Apart in the Oven
This is a result of underproofing. Let your brioche proof slightly longer next time and this issue should resolve itself.

The Brioche Bakes Flat or Collapses Inward after Baking
There are three possible causes for this: undermixing, improper shaping, or overproofing. If you do not develop a strong enough gluten network in your dough, it will not have the structure needed to rise properly in the oven, resulting in a flattened pancake of a bun. Make sure you test your dough using the windowpane test (see page 37). If you passed the windowpane test and still have this issue, make sure you are getting a little bit of tension in your dough when you shape it. The exterior should feel taut as opposed to slack when you're done shaping. And if those two things are not the cause, it could be overproofing. If you overproof your dough, the yeast will have nothing left to give when the pastry hits the oven, and instead of getting a nice spring, it will simply flatten. To prevent overproofing, check your brioche 30 minutes earlier, looking for a gentle springing back when you poke it.

Puff Pastry

My Dimensions Don't Match Up with the Book

That's OK! Dimensions can change based on how much you trim off during lamination and how efficiently you roll out the dough. Focus more on getting your dough to the correct thickness rather than the exact dimensions, as the thickness is what really matters.

The Dough Is Tearing While I Roll It Out

Make sure your dough isn't sticking to the counter or the rolling pin. If it sticks at all, it can cause tears in the dough, which will only amplify as you continue to laminate. You don't want so much flour that it doesn't get any traction on the counter, but it definitely shouldn't stick either. This can also be caused by the dough becoming too soft while rolling it out (see the following entry for additional guidance).

The Dough Is Getting Really Soft While I Roll It Out and/or the Butter Is Starting to Smoosh Out of the Dough

If your environment is warm or it takes you a little while to roll the dough out during each fold, the dough may start to warm up. If this happens, simply let it rest in the fridge for at least 10 minutes before continuing. If you find that the 30-minute rest between folds doesn't get the dough block cold enough, you can extend the rest period up to 45 minutes. Just don't go past that time, as the butter may become too brittle.

The Butter Is Showing through the Dough

This can be because the dough got too thin, and once you roll it out, it becomes even thinner, showing butter through it. Focus on getting your layers of dough/butter/dough extremely even during the locking-in phase to combat this.

The Butter Broke into Pieces While Rolling Out

Your butter was too cold when you started. Make sure you can flex your butter as shown on page 17 before you begin. You can't cut corners with this. If it breaks after its fridge rest, either cut the fridge rest by 5 to 10 minutes or check your fridge temp to make sure it's not below 35 degrees F, as that could cause the butter to harden too quickly.

The Final Dough Is Soft and Hard to Work With

Pop it in the fridge for 15 minutes to firm up. You never want to work with warm puff pastry, as the delicate layers of butter can easily be crushed by your fingertips if it's not solid. Since puff pastry is rolled so thin, it warms up very quickly, so if you find yourself struggling with it melting in your hands, just get it cold and try again.

The Butter Leaked Out of My Pastries in the Oven

This again has to do with temperature. Always keep your puff pastry as cold as possible. Work with one piece at a time when shaping, while the others are in the fridge, and always bake from cold, never room temperature pastry. A small amount of butter leakage is normal, but there shouldn't be a pool of it on your baking tray.

Croissant

My Dimensions Don't Match Up with the Book

That's OK! Dimensions can change based on how much you trim off during lamination and how efficiently you roll out the dough. Focus more on getting your dough to the correct thickness rather than the exact dimensions, as the thickness is what really matters.

The Dough Is Slipping Off the Butter Block on the First Turn

This can happen for several reasons. The first reason is the butter is not adhered to the dough enough. Make sure you brush off any excess flour from your butter block and dough before locking the butter in. I usually give it a few good solid whacks with the rolling pin to make sure the dough is really hugging that butter tightly before I begin rolling it out. The second reason this could happen is you are not rolling the dough with enough downward force. Make sure you put some muscle into rolling your dough out so you're rolling not just the top layer of dough but all three layers of dough/butter/dough at the same time. Lastly, if your dough feels very slack and looks like it more than doubled in the fridge overnight, it may have fermented more than you wanted it to. This can make the dough less stiff and cause it to slide off the butter because it's a different texture from the butter. You can let your butter get slightly softer before laminating, but that is risky because if it gets too soft, it will ooze out the sides and/or melt into the dough. The best course of action is to remix your dough, but make sure all ingredients are very cold and it isn't crowded in your fridge overnight, so it can get ample airflow to help arrest fermentation.

The Butter Is Squeezing Out of the Dough When I Roll It Out

Your butter block got too soft! If this happens, there's no fixing it in the moment; just learn for next time. You will still end up with a delicious pastry, just not a perfectly layered croissant. It will be more like an Italian cornetto.

The Dough Is Tearing While I Roll It Out, or It's Sticking to the Table a Lot

Make sure your dough isn't sticking to the counter or the rolling pin. If it sticks at all, it can cause tears in the dough, which will only amplify as you continue to laminate. You don't want so much flour that it doesn't get any traction on the counter, but it definitely shouldn't stick either.

The Butter Broke While Rolling the Dough Out

Your butter was too cold when you started. Make sure you can flex your butter as shown on page 17 before you begin. You can't cut corners with this. If it breaks after its fridge rest, either cut the fridge rest by 5 to 10 minutes or check your fridge temp to make sure it's not below 35 degrees F, as that could cause the butter to harden too quickly.

I Have Areas Where There Is No Butter in My Dough Book

This is a common occurrence when you're first learning to laminate. Try trimming more off from your turns next time. A game I play against myself at the bakery is to get the smallest amount of just-dough trimmings during my turns. It's a never-ending battle but a fun challenge to work on.

The Dough Springs Back When I Try to Roll It Out

Give it a rest! No, literally, let the dough rest in the fridge to relax a little bit. It's full of tension from getting rolled out and folded so many times, so a little nap will make all the difference.

I Can't Get the Dough to Roll Out into a Rectangle Shape and/or It's Uneven

This just comes from practice with a rolling pin. I prefer to use a handleless straight pin for the best leverage and consistency. French rolling pins, with their tapered ends, tend to make doughs uneven, and the kind with handles do not let you get enough downward leverage. Focus on getting the dough to the correct dimension in at least one way. For example, for the pillar croissant recipe, make sure you get the dough to 13 inches wide and a little less than ¼ inch thick. It won't matter too much if the length of 32 inches doesn't match up.

I'm Not Getting the Yield Suggested

That's OK! My yields are based on doughs I made, laminated, and trimmed myself, and yours will be made, laminated, and trimmed by you, so there's bound to be some variation in how much dough you're left with at the end of the process. If you trim off a larger portion of dough than I do during the first or second turn, you'll have less dough at the end. No biggie!

All the Butter Leaked Out When I Baked the Pastry

This is a classic case of underproofing. Let your pastries proof longer next time.

The Croissants Came Out Dense and Small

Another indicator of underproofing. Let your pastries proof longer next time.

The Croissant Dough Tore When It Proofed

This is usually an indicator of underdeveloped gluten, or it could also be because the butter was too close to the surface of the dough, i.e., uneven lamination. Make sure when you roll your croissant dough up into an egg shape after mixing that it has a smooth surface. If it's very craggy, it may be undermixed, in which case you'll have to throw it back in the mixer for a few minutes. To prevent uneven lamination, really focus on getting your dough/butter/dough extremely even during the locking-in phase, and prioritize rolling all three layers out at once instead of smooshing only the top layer of dough.

The Bottoms of My Pastries Got Too Dark before They Were Cooked in the Middle

My home oven gave me some issues with this, and the way I got around it was to put a piece of aluminum foil underneath the baking sheet. Always bake in the center of your oven so that the heat source is radiant instead of blasting the pan.

The Classic-Shaped Croissants Unraveled in the Oven or during Proofing

This can happen if you do not properly tuck the tail underneath the pastry during shaping or if you have a very fat middle of the pastry that pushes the pastry apart during proofing. When shaping, make sure the dough is of even thickness throughout so you don't end up with a fat middle, and tuck the tail of the croissant all the way under it. It can even poke out the back side a little bit if you want to be on the extra safe side.

My Croissants Baked Flat

A classic sign of overproofing. Check on them earlier next time, and once they jiggle like Jello, they're ready for the oven!

Acknowledgments

I would like to thank all the many people who helped make this book possible. First, to my husband, who has been a never-ending source of encouragement and support throughout this and many other projects I've taken on. Next, to Elaina Stackhouse and Tiffany Wagner, who believed in my vision enough to follow me to the commissary in West Seattle, and who have been there for me to lean on, laugh with, and grow with as professionals together at Temple. To Barry Faught, for his eternally optimistic outlook and seeing the diamond in the rough. Thank you to Ian Wismann-Horther for the use of his recipe; to Richard Peterson, Kristen Thomson, Maddie Geis-Neri, Patrick Sikes, and Jessica Aceti for testing these recipes for me; to Jill Saginario and copyeditor Bridget Sweet for guiding me from idea to final product; to Amber Fouts for capturing my work in the most flattering light; to Francisco Migoya for his ongoing mentorship and support; and finally to all the employees of Temple Pastries for letting me be their leader and being as excited about and dedicated to pastry, bread, and hospitality as I am.

Resources

Equipment

BRIOCHE À TÊTE PANS Nonstick 3-inch fluted molds, BakeDeco.com

COOKIE CUTTERS Stainless steel sets that range from 1 inch to 4½ inches in diameter found widely online

LOAF PAN 9-by-4-by-4 inch USA Pan, found at specialty kitchen shops such as Crate & Barrel

PERFORATED SILPAT Demarle Silpain, BakeDeco.com

RING MOLDS For Kouign Amann, 4-by-2-inch ring molds from Fat Daddio's at BakeDeco.com

Ingredients

CAVIAR Upscale grocery stores or RealGourmetFood.com

DOUBANJIANG Asian grocers or online

DUCK FAT Local butchers, an upscale grocery store or RealGourmetFood.com

FURIKAKE Asian grocers

LABNEH Mediterranean markets, some farmers' markets

MICRO BASIL Farmers' markets, health food stores, or locally in Seattle from Farmbox Greens

NDUJA Specialty Italian markets or gourmet grocers

PANDAN EXTRACT Butterfly Pandan Extract Flavoring, Amazon.com, or some Asian grocery stores

PASSIONFRUIT PUREE Les Vergers Boiron or Perfect Puree, on Amazon.com or WebstaurantStore.com

QUINCE Farmers' markets, some Asian grocery stores

RASPBERRY POWDER Just Raspberry powder, shopkarensnaturals.com

RASPBERRY PUREE Les Vergers Boiron or Perfect Puree, on Amazon.com or WebstaurantStore.com

SUMAC Upscale grocery stores or Mediterranean markets

Index

About the Author

CHRISTINA WOOD is the founder, owner, head chef, and benevolent leader of Temple Pastries. She learned to bake in her home kitchen after graduating from University of Florida with a degree in business management. Professionally, she worked under Coupe du Monde de la Boulangerie winner William Leaman and James Beard-nominated baker James Miller before starting Temple Pastries as a croissant pop-up in 2018. Temple Pastries opened its doors as a brick and mortar in 2020. When she's not at the bakery, she practices Muay Thai, dotes on her cats, and watches *Jeopardy!* with her husband at their home in Seattle.

Printed in China

SASQUATCH BOOKS with colophon is a registered trademark of Blue Star Press, LLC

29 28 27 26 25   9 8 7 6 5 4 3 2 1

The authorized representative in the EU for product safety and compliance is Authorised Rep Compliance Ltd, 3rd Floor, 71 Lower Baggot Street, Dublin D02 P593, Ireland. www.arccompliance.com

ISBN: 978-1-63217-550-2

Editor: Jill Saginario
Designers: Tony Ong and Alison Keefe
Production Editor: Peggy Gannon
Copyeditor: Bridget Sweet
Photographer: Amber Fouts

Sasquatch Books
1325 Fourth Avenue, Suite 1025
Seattle, WA 98101

SasquatchBooks.com

Library of Congress Cataloging-in-Publication Data

Names: Wood, Christina (Pastry chef), author. | Fouts, Amber, photographer.
Title: Pastry temple: baking with inspired flavors / Christina Wood ; photography by Amber Fouts.
Description: Seattle, WA: Sasquatch Books, [2025] .
Identifiers: LCCN 2024054020 | ISBN 9781632175502 (hardcover) | ISBN 9781632175519 (ebk)
Subjects: LCSH: Pastry. | LCGFT: Cookbooks.
Classification: LCC TX773 .W778 2025 | DDC 641.86/5--dc23/eng/20241205
LC record available at https://lccn.loc.gov/2024054020

The recipes contained in this book have been created for the ingredients and techniques indicated. Neither publisher nor author is responsible for your specific health or allergy needs that may require supervision. Nor are publisher and author responsible for any adverse reactions you may have to the recipes contained in the book, whether you follow them as written or modify them to suit your personal dietary needs or tastes.